Nathan,
USE the tools!
ENJOY!

OUTBOUNDING

WILLIAM "SKIP" MILLER

OUTBOUNDING

END YOUR DEPENDENCE ON INBOUND LEADS

HarperCollins
Leadership

An Imprint of HarperCollins

To those who try to overcome their fears.
Little successes lead to big accomplishments.

Published by HarperCollins Leadership, an imprint of HarperCollins Focus LLC.

Book design by Aubrey Khan, Neuwirth & Associates

Any internet addresses, phone numbers, or company or product information printed in this book are offered as a resource and are not intended in any way to be or to imply an endorsement by HarperCollins Leadership, nor does Harper-Collins Leadership vouch for the existence, content, or services of these sites, phone numbers, companies, or products beyond the life of this book.

ISBN 978-1-4002-1945-2 (eBook)
ISBN 978-1-4002-1944-5 (HC)

Library of Congress Control Number: 2020942665

Printed in the United States of America
20 21 22 23 LSC 10 9 8 7 6 5 4 3 2 1

CONTENTS

PART 1—THE STARTING POINT

PART 2—GETTING TO WORK

PART 3—ON YOUR MARK, GET SET . . .

PART 4—GO

PART 5—SALES MANAGEMENT

ACKNOWLEDGMENTS

Thanks to HarperCollins; you folks are the best. Thanks, Tim, for getting this all done, especially with an author who has some good ideas and can't write. (It's why I married a journalism major.)

Thanks to my customers. You folks always ask tough questions and keep me on my game. Outbounding is an art and a science, and with your help, we captured some best practices.

Thanks to those I interviewed and got some best practices from. You are really at the top of your field, and you gave me some great insights. Thanks, Michael, Steven, Christina, Elizabeth, Sean, Melissa, Quinn, Dave, Greg, Dan, Kristen, Nate, all of you.

Thanks to my family. Yes, all fifty-five of you who show up every year for the clambake and Thanksgiving. GOT (Gang of Twelve), you are the best! To my kids, a dad could never be as proud as I am of you three. You guys are all rock stars—all independent, with a competitive will, and an understanding that listening will get you further than talking.

Susie, my wife, you inspire me. You overcome adversity every day with a smile and a laugh.

To my readers, I hated prospecting/outbounding when I was in sales. Fear of rejection. My ego couldn't take a no. I was not good at it at all. I had to learn the hard way. Maybe that helped.

If I had to do it all over again, I would jump in, get dirty, and learn. So, here, in this book, is what I wish I would have learned when I was getting started.

FOREWORD

I'm sure you're familiar with the 211 phenomena: At 211 degrees, water is hot, but increase the temperature by just one degree, to 212, and that same water is boiling. And the by-product of that water, steam, can do amazing things.

Turns out, steam is also an essential part of sales organizations. And you can find it in *Outbounding*.

I've learned from experience that if a company adopts an outbounding culture, its opportunities for success can multiply far beyond optimistic expectations.

As the former vice president of worldwide sales at WebEx, I was in a unique position to create a web-touch model for our go-to-market strategy. We employed a few hundred salespeople and, with Skip's help, became the dominant global solution for video conferencing, online meetings, screen share, and webinars. I think 100x growth and a successful IPO is a good endgame.

We had similar successes at Affectiva and RingCentral. Next up was Zoom, and as president, we really hit the go-to-market model out of the park. Yes, in all these companies we had an assist from sales development representatives (SDRs) with great inbounding efforts. However, if you want to know what really helped step on the gas for Zoom, WebEx, and RingCentral, it was outbounding. That's where we turned hot water into steam.

You can make 80 percent of what you want to achieve with great inbounding efforts, but if you and your company want to really break through what you think is possible, to really hit the impossible, you need to outbound. It's there that you'll find that extra 1 percent that can catapult your sales organization to a whole new level.

I'm now helping small start-up companies to do just that, and I'm bringing Skip with me as much as I can. From WebEx to Zoom, Skip's sales model and his passion for selling are contagious—and they work. His tools are easy to understand, can be implemented quickly, and more important, managers can coach to them. Their beauty is in their simplicity.

Outbounding should not be something anyone puts on the back burner and "will get around to it." By that time, it's probably too late. I think three IPOs proves that.

Skip's newest book shows you how to turn your organization's outbounding efforts into steam. You'll learn his tools, methods, and tips. Listen well, they are different from what you will usually hear, especially outbounding to the C-Suite, or Above the Line, as Skip puts it.

Enjoy what he has to say. I know you'll be pleasantly shocked at how just a few of his tools can make a big difference.

—DAVE BERMAN

Operating Partner, Spider Capital

Former President, WebEx, RingCentral, and Zoom Communications

PREFACE

While writing this book, I have always tried to keep you, the reader, in mind. I think of how lost I felt when I first started in sales with no one to help me prospect.

I remember one day, I had to go to the Anaheim Convention Center and go booth to booth asking for the vice president of marketing. We were selling small trade shows and conferences and were looking for companies that would rent a six-foot table for a day. We figured if they spend the big bucks at these major shows, they probably had some extra money to do local follow-up shows.

I got there at 10:00 a.m. Walked up to the first booth, turned around, went and had a cup of coffee (liquid courage). At 11:00 a.m., went to a booth, asked for the VP of marketing. I was told he was not in yet. Went to the second booth, looked around, and didn't even ask for anyone. I left shortly thereafter. Rejection.

OK, I eventually learned to prospect. I had to do it when I started my own company. It wasn't easy for me, but I learned. So can you.

When I did get some success, I pitched and hoped. Geez. I still remember pitching to the senior vice president (SVP) of Worldwide Purchasing at BFGoodrich with more than a hundred slides, all about us. I had screenshots of our software as slides. Cringe.

This is not a book on how to be a great SDR, salesperson, or how to implement a prospecting system. It's about you, the individual contributor and manager, on how to get results, both strategically and tactically.

As a manager, I was all about execution. Planning is great, but if I can do something, be 80 percent successful, fix the 20 percent and be 80/20 on that, that's 96 percent successful. Where I came from, 96 to 100 percent was an A-plus. I'll take it and let someone else worry about the 4 percent I didn't get.

Outbounding is not going to tell you what technology tools you need to use and buy. By the time this book gets to you, the technology roadmap will have changed, and companies we thought were winners will have withered. Go figure.

What this book will show you is what works and what doesn't through my lens. Do research on this topic like I have done and, wow, there are a lot of people's opinions.

However, with my market research background and the analytical way I think, trends do start to emerge. I like trends. They take time to change, and you can actually see them morph, so really what you see are emerging best practices.

As always, I try to "toolize" some of the tactics so you can use them a piece at a time, rather than eat the whole elephant at once.

ProActiveOutbounding.com has some tools and templates you can use for free. Make sure you put your own voice on the templates. If you just copy and paste, it will not come across sincere, and then you'll blame me when the tools don't work. They work— my customers scream that they do. Use the tools. Be genuine. Use your own words.

Finally, it's about one shoe at a time. Get out of bed and try one thing, keep doing it, and pretty soon it will be a habit. That's how you start.

If you cannot do great things,
do small things in a great way.   —Napoleon Hill

THE PROBLEM

In good economic times, customers are open to buying. They need to buy to fuel growth. Social media and marketing lead generation efforts have been doing a great job driving leads to companies' sales teams. The need for growth coupled with advanced marketing lead generation technology has created the perfect storm.

The concept of inbound marketing wasn't born until 2005, after the phrase was coined by HubSpot's co-founder and CEO, Brian Halligan. It began to show up in tiny blips and bleeps on the internet in 2007, but it wasn't until 2012 that it really started to grow.

The inbound sales efforts (follow up on inbound leads) have now become 40 to 100 percent of a company's sales-lead-generation efforts.

However, as companies have farmed these "early adopters," the easy inbound leads are drying up, and the "low-hanging fruit" has started to disappear. Marketing and social media efforts are not yielding the results they previously attained.

Lay on top of that the growth of the sales department. They hired a lot of people to keep up on the inbound leads and may have too many salespeople now chasing the same or fewer inbound leads than they had before.

Companies are now forced to increase their outbounding or prospecting efforts to meet increasing quotas, by both inside and outside teams.

However:

▸ Inbound sales teams have never been trained how to generate an outbound lead. They have been successful following up on leads, which is what they were taught to do. There is a big difference.

▸ Companies are not training their reps on outbound activities. They do not have the skills.

▸ Outbound salespeople have become so dependent on Sales/Business Development Reps (SDRs or BDRs), their outbound skills have atrophied, and they have not been educated on many of the available tools and processes.

▸ Outbound salespeople acknowledge they will need to generate "20 percent" of their quota on their own, but still do not have a process to outbound, since "It's only 20 percent and I'll find that somewhere." Right, but not by sending out one email every three weeks.

▸ Salespeople and managers do not consider the new buyer's journey—the highly educated inbound buyer—when they are outbounding and "miss the mark." Outbound prospects don't know they don't know. Salespeople still, however, "show up and throw up" in their outbounding attempts. Doesn't work. It's about customer change before customer adoption.

▸ Sales managers are still managing to the "inbound lead/ flip to an account executive" model and have not incorporated the skills or tools to adapt to an outbound sales process, nor do they possess the sense of urgency to do so.

THE CHALLENGE

If you are an inbound salesperson going outbound, an outbound rep who will have to start prospecting, or a dedicated outbound rep, you've noticed that the buy/sales process has changed over time.

With the information buyers have at their disposal, changing economic times, the speed of change, and technology advancements (can you say "AI"?), the outbound sales process has changed. Inbound and outbound sales processes are different.

▸ Inbound sales—the buyer has identified a need, has initiated contact, and has an idea of how to satisfy their "need."

▸ Outbound sales—the buyer has not identified a need yet, has not initiated contact, sometimes doesn't know he or she has a problem, has to be shown a need, and then has to be led through a process.

Most sales processes and the ways managers coach their salespeople have not, unfortunately, taken advantage of this difference. Unbelievable as it may seem, they still think a sale is a sale. How do we know? It's rare that I see two different sales processes in a company. Everyone agrees that outbound and inbound are two different sales, but do they map it, sell to it, and coach to it. Nope. Salespeople still:

▸ Do very little homework—they didn't need to with an inbound lead.

▸ Stay too low in the prospect's organization during the sales process.

▸ Pitch their products—this is what they have been trained to do.

▶ Confirm interest and offer proof, then lose control—demos, trials, proof of concept (POC), send proposal—when you give/send something, not give/get something, you lose control.
▶ Try to get a deal in by the end of month/quarter by discounting the heck out of the deal.

Managers still:

▶ Ignore what is happening in early stages of a sale—they just want prospecting numbers.
▶ Live with 40 to 50 percent forecast accuracy.
▶ Never coach to lead qualification skills. They would rather coach a deal across the finish line.
▶ Focus on what the salesperson is doing—not what the customer is doing.
▶ Make sure the proposal is complete—called selling proposals.
▶ Focus "the" customer value proposition instead of the two that are there.
▶ Offer discounts to get the deal in for the month/quarter.
▶ Assume a "I can do more than the rep" approach and help "close" the deal.

THE NEW OUTBOUND SALES PARADIGM

Outbounding will:

▶ Identify what has changed from a buyer's perspective in a sales process.

▶ Show what skill sets are now needed from inside/ outside salespeople to be effective at outbounding.

▶ Give sales management the ability to identify what skills need to be changed.

▶ Develop new dashboards that will yield higher results.

▶ Recognize what new sales processes need to be adapted and coached to.

Tools and Tactics

Too many prospecting books leave managers and salespeople with the sense that "It was a good read, but what do I do now?"

Here's what you do: For salespeople, you need to really understand your prospects—why they need to change and how to help them see the need to change rather than why they want to buy. It's two different motivations, and it starts with good homework skills.

Except for tire kickers, of course, inbound leads have already accepted the need for change, and they are in a buy process already. You need to work with them in their process and get a decision. They may decide yes or no, but they are headed for some decision.

In an outbound sales situation, clients may:

▶ Have no concept that they need to change.

▶ Know they need to change but have no energy.

▶ Know they need to change but have not started down that path yet.

▶ Have started down the change path informally.

▶ Have started down the path formally.

▶ Be involved with a process to make a change.

▶ Be working with vendors.

▸ Have selected vendors.
▸ Have made a final decision.

There are many subcategories here as well, but look at the difference. An inbound lead already has a head start on an outbound lead.

Client Action	Inbound	Outbound
Identified Need	X	
We May Need to Change—No Energy (Tire Kicking)	X	X
We Need to Change—Just Thinking	X	X
We May Need to Change—Yes Energy to Change	X	X
Started Change Informally	X	X
Started Change Formally	X	
Have Process for Change	X	
Started Working with Vendors	X	
Started Selecting Vendors	X	
Final Decision Made	X	

There is a big difference in the inbound and outbound model. In the outbound model, you may need to address a prospect who does not have a need identified yet. Go ahead, make a sales pitch to someone who doesn't know they don't know.

Outbounding is different than how you would address a prospect who has a formally identified need. Let's assume something here.

An Identified Need prospect is very different than one who has a
Need to Start a Change prospect. The goal in outbounding is not
to sell your stuff yet. The goal is to get them to agree there is a need
for a change.

Look at all the elements that an inbound lead could have accomplished before it contacts a vendor. This substantiates the
idea that the buyer's journey is 40 to 60 percent complete before
contacting a vendor theory.

▶ Outbound—you usually have to identify a need for a
  change and help the prospect start the change process
  with you in control.
▶ Inbound—the change process has happened, and you
  need to get onboard and try to control the buy/sales
  cycle.

The problem with this assumption is that most salespeople
want to sell something when they outbound, which is admirable,
but not where the customer is.

An inbound prospect is engaged in the need for change, and
most sales efforts start off with this energy. An outbound prospect
can be anywhere along this model, and therefore a salesperson
needs to assess, align, and message accordingly. The guesswork
for this effort needs to be taken out of the area of magic and
moved into a sales-prospecting effort.

For managers, the need to organize and manage these variables is huge. The days of "go out and bang on a few doors" are
over. No more doughnut drops. The need to have a prospecting
process that a manager can measure, coach to, and create rewards
over is now upon us. It's a complex problem that needs simple,
coachable answers.

It's not rocket science. It is a process, and the quality of the sales effort surely triumphs over quantity. Sending a thousand emails out hoping three stick is not the way to do it anymore. Attempting a hundred calls, hoping to get someone on the phone who will talk to you, can work, but what a waste of time and resources.

Sure, sales is a numbers game, but the quality of the message, attempts, and targets are probably more important than pure numbers. Spam filters, caller ID, and gatekeepers are getting better and better.

So, here is where the science and art of outbounding/prospecting are at your disposal. Outbounding has always been part of the job. Some used to call it prospecting, cold-calling, or hitting the streets. Some still do.

Outbounding implies prospecting with more available tools.

You may like it, although, as salespeople will admit, most don't. That's because most are doing it wrong, getting rejected, and then rationalizing why outbounding is something you know you should get to, but really, you would rather poke yourself in the eye with a pencil than cold call and outbound. Plus, you're probably doing it wrong.

Give outbounding a chance. Learn how to do it, enjoy it, and change the way you sell. Your quota is going up next year. You have to make it. Hope is not enough.

PART 1

The Starting Point

Emails that contain questions are 50 percent more likely to get replies than emails without any questions.

CHAPTER 1

The Story

JERRY AND JENNIFER are talking. They have been friends for a long time, really neighbors, and even though they both are busy and in sales, they usually have a coffee every few weeks just to stay in touch.

Jennifer got into sales after attending a neighborhood block party. Jerry and Jennifer got to talking, and Jerry convinced her that sales were in her cards. Jerry would act as a coach and mentor if she wanted to get into sales. She had just been laid off from her current job and had nothing to lose. Jennifer agreed, and the rest, as they say, is history.

Today, they are sort of talking and complaining. Jerry is a senior account executive (SAE) for the ABC company, a marketing automation software company, and Jennifer is a senior sales development rep (SDR) for the XYZ company, a shop-floor machine-tool vendor.

"No, you're wrong. I've got it much tougher," Jerry spoke out. He was pretty adamant. Seems like they were having a discussion on whose job was getting harder.

"I'm tracking to be about 85 percent of goal YTD," he said. "With my current pipeline and with the lack of good leads the SDR team is sending over right now, I'll have to do some out-bounding myself, even though it's not my job. Seems like I have to do everything myself."

Jennifer was having none of it. "Well, Jerry, you are really wrong on this one. At least you have a territory and customers you can prospect into. We have been told we have to generate 20 percent more leads than we have been sending over, and the only way to reach those new goals is to outbound, which we have never been trained to do, and quite frankly, is not in my job description. I follow up on inbound leads, qualify for fit, and then flip them over to sales or out of the funnel. That's my job. I don't understand why I have to change what I do every day just because the company isn't getting enough good inbound leads. They should make the AEs go find some leads. Isn't that why they call them hunters?"

The last few months for both ABC and XYZ have been kind of rocky. It looks like they both will miss revenue forecasts for the quarter, and that hasn't happened at either company for many years. Both companies are feeling the pressure and salespeople are getting a bit on edge.

In both companies, management has been sending a strong message—*Let's fill the funnel so we have prospects we can attempt to bring in by the end of the quarter, now, whatever it takes.*

"Listen, Jen, I know it seems like an impossible task, but you just have to call lists and make dials. That's what I did when I started out. In my current role, I have to generate interest, control the sales process, and then close deals to make money. Closing is hard work, so now I have to add prospecting to my list of to-do's and, well, it just seems like I'm not getting any help.

"The number of leads I'm getting has dropped significantly, and now I'm getting terrible quality leads, I mean, Facebook leads for a B2B sale, really?" Jerry was frustrated, and it was coming out in his tone.

Jennifer was on a roll, though, and nothing was going to stop her.

"I've been at my company for almost two years now," she said, "and I've never had to outbound. Following up on inbound traffic is what I was hired to do and I'm pretty good at it. Now, I've got to cold-call, cold-email, sequence my contacts, set cadences, and on and on. It's just not attractive. I hate getting rejected. It's why I took this job and turned down an AE job. Outbounding is just not what I do."

SUMMARY

Conversations like this are happening more and more often. Inbound traffic for sales leads, given the advancement in marketing, has done a great job over the years. Website hits, blogs, conferences, referrals, and digital apps have made it simple to get leads . . . when a buyer initiates the interest.

Research has shown that a buyer who generates interest is already down a buy path and is therefore a more qualified lead than one where you have to generate a need.

Inbound, except for tire kickers who can be disqualified quickly, usually have an identified need and the deal has energy, since the prospect is open to change. That's why they are dedicating some resource to explore the situation.

When outbounding, the prospect could be anywhere on the buyer's journey. They:

1. May not know they need anything.
2. May not know they need to change.
3. May know they need something, or need to change, but it's not a priority yet.
4. May know they need something and are just starting to investigate.
5. Are in full investigation mode, and they did not contact you (you're not driving the sale, someone else is).
6. Are making a decision and need to validate a few other vendors, usually on price.
7. Made a decision and now there is no need.

There are more categories to be sure, but let's compare.

Inbounding to get a lead is just like hopping on a bus that has already been identified, qualifying you are on the right bus, and then going through a buy/sales process, hopefully with you in control.

Outbounding, to get a lead, you may have to:

1. Find out if they are looking for a bus.
2. Figure out if there really is a need to change buses.
3. Help develop what the new bus needs to do.
4. Help the clients generate the energy for getting a new bus.
5. Help the clients work out whether they can afford a new bus.
6. Help the clients figure out what the new bus is going to do that the old bus didn't.
7. Create a plan of how to implement the bus.

You get the point.

Or, you can outbound to see if a prospect has an ongoing process and you just have not been contacted yet, which usually means someone else is driving the bus and, well, that deal is going to come down to price, isn't it? Are you feeling shopped yet?

Either way, outbounding requires skills people have not acquired and managers have not been made aware how to coach, measure, and reward for it.

Welcome. There is a better way.

CHAPTER 2

→

How Do Customers Buy?

I have no special talent.
I am only passionately curious.   —Albert Einstein

WHY IS IT that most salespeople try to sell something, be it a solution, a process, a platform, a service, a product, or an intangible? Whatever it is, wouldn't it be easier to get customers to buy rather than try to sell them something? If customers have already agreed to make a change in how they currently are doing things, getting them to buy something is usually a layup (basketball term, sorry).

When outbounding, the attitude you take every day to every call, email, and touch must be with the customer in mind, not what you want to do.

• • •

THE START

When you look at how someone buys something, look no further than emotional needs and wants. It can be argued that at the consumer level, fears, needs, love, safety, and the like most often drive consumer behavior. Years ago, an article in *Inc.* magazine said there are some basic emotional reasons people buy.

Greed. "If I make a decision now, I will be rewarded."

Fear. "If I don't make a decision now, I'm toast."

Altruism. "If I make a decision now, I will help others."

Envy. "If I don't make a decision now, someone else will win."

Pride. "If I make a decision now, I will look smart."

Shame. "If I don't make a decision now, I will look stupid."

Not going to argue these, and in a Business to Consumer (B2C) world, that works out quite well. Now compare these typical reasons a company buys something.

▶ Revenue Increase—Revenue drives the company, and getting things out of the way to help achieve revenue is usually the top motivator.
▶ Cost Reduction—Getting rid of costs so the company can spend the money it has on more revenue-generating ideas; also called "improvements" or "efficiencies."

▸ Market Share—Market share grabs are not for the weak, but you see time and time again where spending freely to capture market can pay out at the end.

▸ Risk Reduction—At the ATL (Above the Line) level, it is all about risk. Help a company to address risk issues, thus making them money or saving them some.

▸ Market Speed—Usually, the faster you can respond to market needs, the more money you can make.

▸ Quality Improvement—Technology, among other options, is a big sale here. Customer churn, repeat customers, and the ability to attract customers away from the competition are reasons usually put into this bucket.

▸ Personal—People buy from people they like and trust; see "risk reduction" above.

Warren Buffett constantly preaches that profitable growth is *the* mission of a company. Without profitable growth (value investing), a company will surely die.

OK, you now know the drivers for why a company would make a purchase, but what about the drivers? What motivates a company to buy? What motivates a company to change?

THE CUSTOMER—WHY BUY?— THE NEED FOR CHANGE

The great thing about business is things change. Without change, a business will not last. It won't be able to compete. It has to consistently change or it will lose whatever advantage it has to competitors. Without change, there would be no need for a company to answer your outbound sales emails.

Most companies need to change to stay competitive. Market demands, changing consumer preferences, and innovations require companies to constantly reassess what it offers and how it offers it.

One theory suggests there are three elements of change:

1. Knowing what you need to stop doing
2. Knowing what you need to start doing
3. Knowing how to keep the change process alive to keep innovating and taking risks

This theory suggests when companies need to change, they need help on getting to where they need to go. They may have a lack of knowledge, which is why they might seek out a vendor to help them get to where they need to go, a classic make or buy decision.

With change as a necessary way of life in business, Gallup asserts that 70 percent of all change initiatives fail. That's a 30 percent success rate. Ouch.

Buyers usually need help with their changes. Oh, by the way:

1. No one likes to change (it's why you use the same toothpaste and soap you used when you were a kid).
2. Change is hard.
3. Change is a process (yep, got you on that one).

To add more gas to the fire, if change does not have enough energy, it will surely not obtain the desired effect. A classic analogy is a roller coaster—if it doesn't have enough energy at the beginning of the ride, it will not get over the hill.

Your outbounding strategy must consider change when you are outbounding, especially when you are doing your homework. It's something the customer must do, but they hate to do it, it's risky, and they are not good at it. There are two theories about where energy to change comes from, bottom up and top down.

Bottom-Up Theory—In a bottom-up change world, change comes from the market, the workers, or lower-level employees. Top leaders in the company must listen to the employees, the market, the customers, and help facilitate change. To get real change, the bottom-up folks need to be heavily involved, since they are the ones who will be implementing change. A bottom-up approach is usually a longer process than a top-down approach, but with the ability to get consensus, usually things get done.

A good example of a bottom-up-change process is employee satisfaction and customer satisfaction surveys. The company is asking for input and is looking for things it may not be aware of when it wants to make a change. We work with a few companies that have a technology that offers to help companies facilitate this need for bottom-up change.

Top-Down Theory—A top-down approach to change can be effective when time is critical. Usually in a top-down approach, lower-level workers are told of the change and are expected to get onboard, which usually leads to communication gaps and possible resentment, also called the "not invented here" syndrome.

Most reorganizations are top down, where senior management figures out the best go-to-market (GTM) strategy needed going forward, creates new organization charts, and then announces to all what the new organization looks like and where everybody will sit. Most entrepreneurial start-ups are top down. The vision of the founder.

Both theories have their strengths and weaknesses, and the need to change, bottom up or top down, will create a need for buyers to open their doors to vendors if what they need to accomplish (goals and initiatives) cannot be met with current processes or equipment/tools.

MOTIVATION TO CHANGE

The need for change will exist in most companies if they want to succeed. Change must be a process, not a single event if it is to be successful. It's important to understand change if you want to be successful at outbounding, since energy to take an outbounding salesperson's call is really buried in the prospect's need to change. Understand change, and you will have a leg up on your outbound messaging.

One of the best explanations of a change process comes from psychologist Kurt Lewin.

▶ **Lewin Change Model**

Lewin suggested change is a process and it must go through three stages to be successful: unfreezing, changing, and re-freezing.

Change requires that the need, or the perception of the need, to change has been identified. The goal is a new, desired level of change (the process of change), and then finally, solidifying that behavior as the new way of doing things. Start with a block, have a vision of the cone, and know you need to implement change to get there.

Unfreezing

Before a change can be implemented, it must go through the initial step of unfreezing. Because many companies and executives will naturally resist change, the goal during the unfreezing stage is to create an awareness of how the current state is hindering the organization. This is called "looking backward," countering the "we've always done it this way" objection.

Old behaviors, ways of thinking, processes, people, and organizational structures must all be looked at, and this is a perfect time to outreach to C-Suite buyers in an organization, but more on that later.

Changing

Change is a process where the organization must transition or move into this new vision. This is a very fluid state, and one where a company is usually looking for an answer, since change is not always 100 percent sure and can fluctuate as the change is in process.

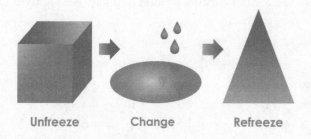

Unfreeze   Change   Refreeze

This changing step, also referred to as "in process," is identified by the implementation of the change. This is where you start looking forward and the change becomes real. It is also a time when companies understand that the tools, systems, or processes they have today are not enough to get them to where they need to be, so it's another good time to reach out to potential buyers. This realization is a time when buyers are looking for solutions to help them solidify their ideas of change.

Refreezing

Refreezing is the act of reinforcing, stabilizing, and solidifying the new vision after the change. The changes made to organizational processes, goals, structure, offerings, or people are accepted and refrozen. Again, the tools or processes needed to reinforce the change may need to be modified, which is where you, the salesperson, can help.

Why go through this change model? It identifies where the buyer is in a process, and where you can direct your communication to be more effective and improve those 6 percent or so open rates of prospecting emails. Again, more later.

Buy/Sales Process

You have all seen the many versions of a buy/sales process. The one we use at M3 Learning is quite popular (see Figure 2.1).

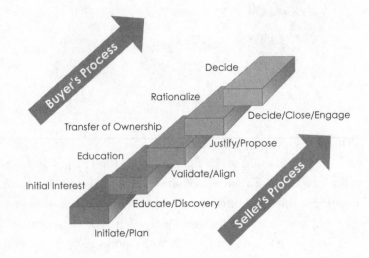

Figure 2.1

This is a very good buy/sales model, but it assumes the buyer's initial interest. It implies that they are interested in something like what you are selling. It assumes a willingness to change and the initial energy to do so. Great for an inbound lead, but from an outbounding perspective, the model needs to add an earlier stage, one that is before initial interest. A Stage 0, if you will (see Figure 2.2).

This preopportunity stage is a buyer's stage where they may or may not know there is a need to change, and the energy and exact need and outcomes desired for the change may have yet to be identified. Effective outbounding here is focused on the need for change, rather than product needs and fit. Find the pain points (I hate that term) and why they may need to change. This is much more effective than the process to educate, present, demo them on your stuff (show up and throw up and hope something sticks), propose, and hope.

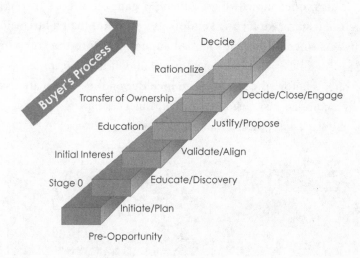

Figure 2.2

Figure 2.3 shows another buyer's process, this one for a technology sale. It progresses quite a bit before any vendor is contacted. There are a lot of questions that a company goes through before it starts making a buy decision, and these questions can be coming from anywhere within the organization.

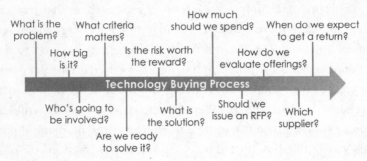

Figure 2.3

This model shows what a buying organization goes through before it starts contacting vendors. It's different than a buy/sales process since it looks at what is happening before the company goes on a buy/sales journey. Bottom line, it looks at quite a few variables before the sale starts to include vendors. These are usually a company asks itself before/during a change.

Figure 2.4 is a model that looks at buying software:

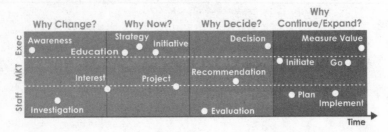

Figure 2.4

The areas of "Why Change?" and "Why Now?" are really buyer-centric because they include the big question, "Why change?"

What help do prospects want in their buying process? The "Why change?" question has to be addressed with the company's buying reasons, in other words, revenue, costs, risks, time, market share, and so on. There always must be a return on an investment for any change, and it must be a measurable return, or no CFO is going to fund it.

HOW COMPANIES BUY— THE BUY-SELL PYRAMID

To blend these models to fit most B2B sales situations, a Buy-Sell Pyramid model represents this need for change well (see Figure 2.5). It includes:

▸ Why Change?—Why do we need to do something different?
▸ Why Now?—What is causing this need for change?
▸ What Is the Outcome Desired?—What is the outcome for the investment required?
▸ What Is the Measured Return (ROI)?—How will we measure success?
▸ Decision to Go Forward—Yes or No?

To really understand where your customer is coming from, work your way up the pyramid to allow you and the prospect to fully uncover the energy, or lack of energy, to change. Ask these questions of the prospect to see where they are so you know what to do.

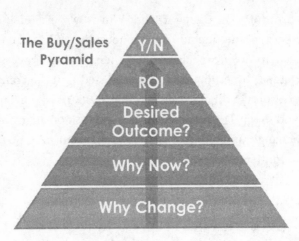

The Buy/Sales Pyramid

Y/N
ROI
Desired Outcome?
Why Now?
Why Change?

Figure 2.5

ATTITUDE AND CONFIDENCE

Before you read on and start using some tools we have developed to outbound, the topics of attitude and confidence have to be mentioned. Years ago, I wrote a book with Ron Zemke called *Knock Your Socks Off Prospecting*. It was a pretty good book. What most people don't know is when I was about halfway through with the book, I scrapped it and started over. I gained a new perspective.

I started over with the knowledge that a salesperson's attitude is probably the most important variable in the outbounding equation. With the attitude of being curious, really trying to understand why the prospect needs to change, and using sales and communication skills, most salespeople will dramatically increase their chance for success. It's not about the sale, it's about the attitude of being curious and finding out why the prospect may need to change.

▸ Being curious—really trying to understand the prospect, not just asking questions to sell your stuff.

▸ Why the prospect needs to change—what has happened in the past or what is about to happen that is causing the prospect to invest time and effort in creating change.

▸ Sales and communication skills—great salespeople are always trying to master their craft, and listening skills, communication skills, and sales-cycle-control skills are extremely important.

▸ It's not what you say, it's how you say it. If you say it confidently, people tend to believe it.

BELIEF

The acceptance that something exists or is true, especially when there is no proof.

Having trust, faith, or confidence in someone or something.

If you believe not only in your abilities, but that you can really help your customer with a change, not merely the belief that your customer needs your product or services, you will succeed more than you will fail. That's the attitude of most of the top outbounding salespeople we interviewed, too.

You need to see things from your customer's chair before you can be effective in selling, period. Master the Buy-Sell Pyramid, have a customer-centric attitude, and believe that your selling, listening, and communication skills will help you get a first jump on this topic of outbounding.

● ● ●

THE STORY

Jennifer and Jerry are still at it, but they have decided to have a contest. They each have set a goal to outbound, and neither one knows they have targeted some of the same accounts. One in particular, the Royal Fireplace Company.

"I'll beat my usual goal and get a 'whale' deal in one week," Jennifer boasted.

"Well, that's pretty conservative of you," Jerry responded. "I'll get five good prospects in the funnel by the end of the month, and that will beat my usual by four, so who is trying harder now?"

"That's all well and good Jerry, but your bark is probably worse than your bite. Let's compare first emails."

"You're not stealing any of my thunder. I know how to prospect," Jerry bellowed.

"Well, with that I'm-good-at-this attitude, you shouldn't be afraid to share, right? Come on, let's see what both of ours look like and compare notes."

"OK, but I know I'll not get any help from what you are doing."

Jerry's prospecting email:

Dear XXXX,

My name is Jerry Davis, and I work for the ABC Company. We recently have come out with some new products and new pricing that you may want to take advantage of.

If you don't know, we are the leader in our industry and have been number one for the past three years. I'm sure you have a need for our platform, everyone needs leads, and now is a great time to take advantage of our low prices.

Please let me know when is a good time for us to connect.

> Jerry Davis
> Sales Executive
> ABC Company

Jennifer's prospecting email:

Dear XXXX,

As the end of the year approaches, you probably are considering changes to your business. Some changes are easy, some hard.

If you are looking to change your go-to-market strategy, we have a really interesting, thought-provoking article, "Next Year's Changes and Risks," that may affect your plans.

I would be happy to send it to you if you are interested. Just reply and it's on its way.

> Jennifer Smith
> Sales Development Rep
> XYZ Corporation

Two different emails. Thinking? Hold that thought.

THREE

What Help Do Prospects Want in Their Buying Process?

More than 40 percent of salespeople say outbounding is the most challenging part of sales.

NOW THAT YOU see how and why customers choose to change and how you may be a part of that change, it's important to know a bit more about what goes on in a customer buy process and how you can be involved.

Have you ever walked into a retail store, and while looking around, the store salesperson asks, "May I help you?"

Your instant response is, "Just looking."

The salesperson is asking to help you without even knowing why you came into the store. That's why you didn't want help; it was all about the salesperson, who never asked about you. It doesn't work in retail, why would it work for you?

THE COMPANIES/INDIVIDUAL BUY MODEL

Going forward, there are some assumptions and golden rules you may want to know.

1.   Companies buy, but it's individuals who make decisions.
2.   There are two decisions in a B2B sale, one below the line (BTL) and one above the line (ATL).

ATL
———
BTL

3.   Typically, an ATL is a vice president or above, and a BTL is a manager or user.
4.   ATL and BTL buyers have different value propositions. In a small business, they may be the same person, but still there are two value propositions.
5.   ATLs need the investment to make a fiscal impact. They have the ability to move budget money around to fund changes, and they need to make a change (energy).
6.   BTLs want whatever they are buying to work better than what they are using now. They receive a budget from an ATL.
7.   BTLs create the decision criteria list, what the change needs to do, since they are the ones ultimately responsible for using it.

8. There typically is an ATL event that causes the ATL to initiate the need for change.
9. The BTLs will drag out a decision without ATL involvement. They want to make sure they get the best one and do the right thing by exploring all options.
10. The ATL will always know the size of the problem and how much you will impact that problem (quantified cause).

To demonstrate this model, let's turn to an example about a company needing to make a change. Here is a narrative that will demonstrate the customer buy/sales process.

THE ROYAL FIREPLACE COMPANY—OVERVIEW

The Royal Fireplace Company has been in business for fifty years. Joe Fellows is the current CEO and has been with Royal for three years. The management team includes:

Joe Fellows—CEO

Cheryl Tell—CFO

Bart Li—CMO

Brian James—VP Engineering/Manufacturing

Linda Hall—Marketing Manager

Bill Jarvis—Manager of Manufacturing

Status

Royal just finished the year at $120 million, a 4 percent increase. The market is growing about 3 percent, so all in all, pretty good. However, new in-wall gas models are growing 80 percent. Royal wants a piece of that new market.

Home remodels are increasing 40 percent. Demand for new fireplace models are soaring, and Royal is missing the boat.

September/October:

Joe and Cheryl have been talking about going after this new market for a while. After an executive off-site, they have reached a decision—Royal is going for it. The goal is to keep the current growth rate on the current models, and, in addition, design, manufacture, and deliver new in-wall gas models. The goal was to finish the year with about $10 million in sales. The second year should double to $20 million.

Two big problems:

1. Current manufacturing capabilities cannot handle the new models. Two new machines are needed and will cost about $100,000 each. Total manufacturing investment will be about $1 million, which includes added headcount and facilities.

2. The current market automation system is not set up for these new models. Royal will need to upgrade its marketing automation tools to create demand and help win over current distributors who are selling the competition. Lead generation, in-store promotions, and new automation tools will cost Royal about $3 million, all in.

Bottom line, Royal needs to invest $4 to $5 million to get $10 million in revenue. At a 40 percent cost of goods sold model, that's $4 to $5 million to get $6 million top-line earnings first year. Close to break even. Year two, though, looks good.

October/November

After the executive off-site, Brian, vice president of engineering/ manufacturing (ATL), has reviewed his goals for next year with Bill, manager of manufacturing (BTL). They include:

1. Hiring three new people.
2. Buying two new machines to handle new production.
3. Using current floor space for these new operations.

Brian has told Bill he will need to hire these new people and get them trained and up and running by July 1, the start of the third quarter. Engineering will have its new designs done well before that.

He also needs to get the two machines he needs on line by June 1.

Bill has sent out some feelers to two different machine-tool vendors for some initial ideas and quotes. His goal is to decide by February.

Bart, CMO (ATL), has reviewed his goals for the next year with Linda, marketing manager (BTL). His needs are:

1. Increase the demand for current products by 4 percent.
2. Generate demand for new products to get top-line sales of $10 million.
3. Create and deliver a marketing campaign for the new models.

Outside of all the other marketing demands, he and Linda have determined they will need to upgrade their current marketing automation system.

After doing a little homework, Linda has determined that the current vendor and possibly one other will meet her needs. She sent out a request to both for more information. She wants to make a decision by the end of the year and have it up and start generating leads by the middle of the second quarter.

Back at the executive suite, Joe is not happy with launching in the summer. "I don't understand why this is taking so long," he challenged his executive team. "Can't we get all this going and launch in the beginning of the second quarter? That will put us on track to start shipping in the third quarter. Delaying until the third quarter puts revenue at risk."

At the end of the day, Joe gets everyone to agree with the end of the first quarter for lead-generation efforts to start, launch at the end of the first quarter, take orders, and start shipping June 1.

He also thinks Marketing is dragging its feet on this new software tool, but he admits it's "not his thing," so he has to defer to Bart and Linda. "I wish they were tied to the top-line revenue goals like I am," he mutters at the end of the off-site.

OK, look at all the opportunity for the sales organizations here.

1. Most vendors will assume that Bill and Linda, both BTL buyers, are the key people, and they will be their "champions."
2. Both vendors will focus on presentations and demonstrations.
3. Both vendors will try to get to Brian and Bart, the ATL line of business (LOB) buyers. If successful, they will probably ask what does the client want in what they are

selling. What key features are they looking for? "What do you want our stuff to do for you?" (Really?)

4. What they won't be asking is why is the client changing, what is the expected outcome for these changes, and if there are any expectations not being met.
5. Ditto if they make contact with Cheryl (CFO) and Joe (CEO). This is called an executive overview of "our stuff" presentation. Really? Talk about a missed opportunity.

Most of the manufacturing equipment and marketing automation sales teams will focus forward:

1. What are you looking for in our stuff?
2. What key features are you looking for?
3. Here's why we are better than the competition.
4. What is your budget?
5. What is your buying process?
6. Do you want a demo?

They will miss:

1. The size of the problem and the revenue upside discussion. This is called a gap. More later.
2. The opportunity to help Royal get to market faster, which would bring in more money and lower the revenue risk.
3. The ability to sell faster. If they tapped into ATL energy, their sales cycle would be cut way down. By just focusing on the BTLs, this deal will take its good ol' time.

4. The opportunity to get the ATL buyers energized by discussing their goals and gaps, which would make the deal happen faster. They will be focusing on the BTL buyers feature/function needs.

Guess what would happen if:

▸ The executive team knew it could get product shipping earlier than June?
▸ The new marketing automation tool could be online by January and start generating leads three months earlier than planned? Can you say "pipeline"?
▸ The risk of getting the $10 million in revenue could be spread out over nine months instead of six? They might even beat the $10 million by 20 percent or so.

What do you think these events could do for Royal's top-line revenue projections, if costs did not increase?

TWO VALUE PROPOSITIONS

As demonstrated in the above story, Royal has two value propositions going for it.

ATL Value Proposition

1. Joe (CEO)—Get revenue faster for new models with less risk.
2. Cheryl (CFO)—Same as Joe.
3. Bart (CMO)—Get leads five months faster, and get leads before product starts shipping. A bonus is that Linda will probably be measured by getting the system

up and running by the first quarter, and if she can get it going by January, she gets two months of leads for free. Guess what that would mean to the overall annual goal? Two months of leads that go into the planned three quarters of lead goals. (How would you like to have the ability to have quota for nine months and get eleven months of leads?)

4. Brian (vice president of engineering/ manufacturing)—Get new machines and onboard new hires without plant disruption.

BTL Value Proposition

1. Linda—Get a state of the art, new marketing-automation system. And eliminate problems caused by the old one that were giving her headaches.
2. Bill—Get new machines so he can do more with the latest technology and be really proud of his shop floor.

So, if this sale has two value propositions, what is the sales cycle (theoretical) for these deals? (See Figure 3.1.)

1. Discovery—Understand what Royal wants to do with what they are buying.

    Marketing automation—"Let us give you a presentation of what we do and why we are the best at it in the marketplace."

    Shop floor machines—"We want to show you what our machine can do and how well it can handle what you want it to do."

2. Demo the software/equipment
3. Propose
4. Harass

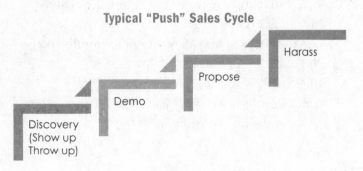

Figure 3.1

Really, that's it? The executive team has a stake in these investments, especially from a revenue and cost standpoint. The most
the sales teams will ask the executives is, "What do you want our
stuff to do for you?"

Once again, "Really, that's it?" That's what the sales team wants
to know? Just the BTL value prop from both the BTL and ATL
buyers? Look at the value and the energy they are leaving on the
table. Amazing. Watch when both start discounting near the end
of the month, too.

They both are missing:

Why is Royal changing?

What are the desired goals and outcomes for this change?

What are the challenges (gaps) in obtaining these goals?

If there weren't any challenges or needs to make this change,
they wouldn't be having to sit through sales pitches. Time to focus
on two value propositions, not just one.

THE QUESTION

Day in and day out, ask a salesperson about the most important deal. We do it all the time.

"Tell us about your key deal for the quarter."

"OK, it's the ABC company, and they want to buy our stuff, and the deal is worth about $150,000. Bob, the BTL buyer, is our champion. He loves us and wants our stuff. We have talked to the ATL buyer, Mary, and she has assured us that this is Bob's decision."

(Of course she did, after you gave her a BTL presentation that lasted an hour and was all about what is interesting to Bob.)

Most salespeople will miss the ATL value proposition, and just sell to the BTL. By doing this, they will commoditize their sale, especially to the ATL ("Don't really care which one we buy . . .") and will have to discount or offer great terms to get the deal. This has to stop.

When outbounding, you will need to know how a customer is being sold to, and that each potential customer's want is different. Outbounding to the ATL and to the BTL have different value propositions. They are coming from two different perspectives.

So here is *The Question*:

Why do you only have one value proposition outbounding template?

Two different buyers. Two different energy sources, and you wonder why you always get pushed down from the C-Suite. Wrong value proposition.

* * *

PRE-MODEL—BUYER'S JOURNEY

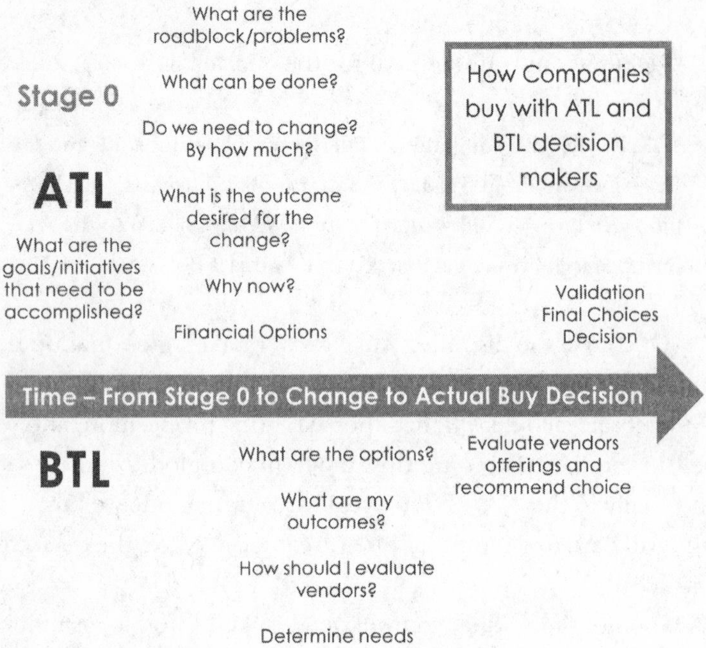

What are the
roadblock/problems?

Stage 0   What can be done?

Do we need to change?
By how much?

ATL   What is the outcome
desired for the
change?

What are the
goals/initiatives
that need to be   Why now?
accomplished?
Financial Options

How Companies
buy with ATL and
BTL decision
makers

Validation
Final Choices
Decision

Time – From Stage 0 to Change to Actual Buy Decision

BTL   What are the options?   Evaluate vendors
offerings and
What are my   recommend choice
outcomes?

How should I evaluate
vendors?

Determine needs

Figure 3.2

The Two Buyers' Journeys—Simple Form

The two buyers' journeys early in the decision process, Stage 0,
are very important in the outbounding world. Before a prospect
contacts a vendor, or will accept a cold call, the motivation will be
as follows:

ATL Buyer—We need to make a change, and the revenue and
cost of this change needs to happen quickly and with as little risk
as possible.

BTL Buyer—Heard we may need to buy some stuff that I might be interested in, so maybe I'll poke around a bit and see what's out there.

You love the second one, since it's all about your favorite topic, you and your stuff. You will be missing the ATL buyer's basic motivations in Stage 0, which you need to exploit.

Maybe a better way to look at this whole thing is to look at a tool called Solution Boxes.

SOLUTION BOXES

As discussed before, there are two value propositions, or two Solution Boxes (see Figure 3.3). For the sake of argument, let's call them Solution Box A and Solution Box B.

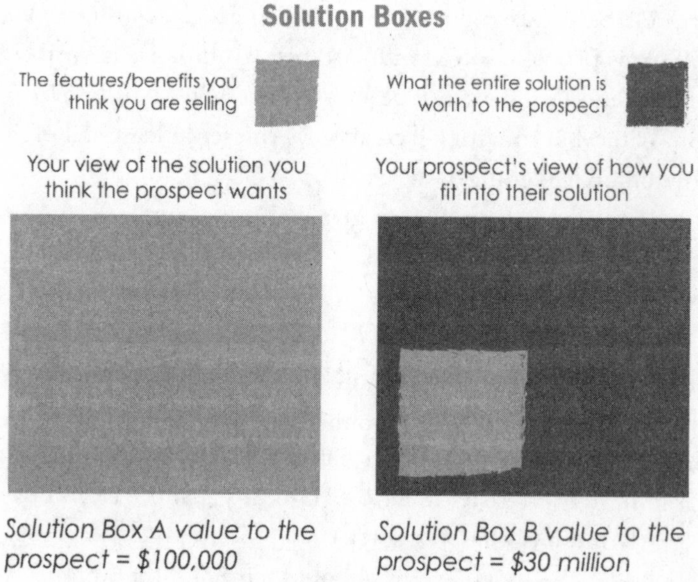

Solution Boxes

The features/benefits you think you are selling

What the entire solution is worth to the prospect

Your view of the solution you think the prospect wants

Your prospect's view of how you fit into their solution

Solution Box A value to the prospect = $100,000

Solution Box B value to the prospect = $30 million

Figure 3.3

With Solution Box A, just figure that is what you are selling, the whole box. Solution Box A says you are the solution, and this is what the BTL buyer really wants—all of what you can sell for what they have in the budget. They have a budgeted amount to spend, in this case, $100,000. If you can show the buyer of Solution Box A, the BTL buyer, you can meet their needs and stay within the size of Solution Box A. *Ta da*, you're done.

Solution Box B is definitely ATL. They have an initiative usually worth millions, in this case $30 million, and they have a few problems with it, which is why they are willing to take your call. If you can make a dent in their Solution Box B so it will make more money, cost less, save time, make it less risky, or solve a problem, you will be extremely necessary to the ATL buyer. You will not be the answer for the entire Solution Box B like you are for Solution Box A. You just have to be part of the solution, and the ATL will tell you how much you are worth.

"Well, Skip, based on what you are offering, I can see at least half of my problem solved with just this. My initiative is worth $30 million, and I think we will be short of this goal (gap) by $10 million. With what you just talked about, I can see at least half of that $10 million gap going away."

Yes, you can get an ATL to give you these numbers, because that's what they do all the time.

Solution Box notes:

1. Both Boxes are important, but ATL only cares about Box B, and BTL only cares about Box A. (Yes, I invented Solution Boxes before ATL/BTL. It would have been easier to have ATL to Box A and BTL to Box B, but it is what it is, sorry.)
2. ATL clients want to talk about their Solution Box B because they have some challenges with it, and if you

can help address some of these challenges, watch how much energy this deal will have.

3. Assume in this case, the ATL buyer feels about 70 percent confident of their $30 million Solution Box B. That means they have a gap of $9 to $10 million (30 percent). If you can make a dent on the $9 to $10 million, say half (number has to come from them), watch how fast this sale picks up speed.

4. For quick, budgeted deals, you may not need to go after Solution Box B, but for those big deals, it's a must have.

SUMMARY

You want to outbound better, but to do that, you need to know why your prospects at the ATL and BTL levels would want to talk to you. This is really important, since it will have you talk less about yourself and have them talk more about themselves.

> ▶ **Sales Law—Best Sales Call in the World**
>
> The best sales call in the world is not one where you leave going: "Boy, was I on my game today. That was a great call."
>
> The best sales call in the world is where you end the call saying, "I never really said anything about us," and the buyer walks away saying, "They heard me, they know exactly what we are trying to do."

THE STORY

It's been a few days, and Jerry is in a foul mood. He has sent out a few emails trying to get some leads, and he thought he had a good one in the Royal Fireplace Company. He had heard Royal was looking to change its marketing automation system, and Jerry is convinced his platform would be perfect, even though he's never talked to Royal.

He sent the marketing manager, Linda Hall, an email, but so far, he has heard nothing. He's going to try email number two.

> Dear Ms. Hall
>
> I sent you an email the other day and have not heard back from you. I know things are busy. Our marketing automation platform is highly regarded. We added more than two hundred new customers this year and are looking for a banner year.
>
> If you would like to "jump onboard," I would love to arrange a quick, fifteen-minute, custom demonstration for your review. When would you like to talk?
>
> Regards,
> Jerry

Jennifer emailed the CEO and the CFO, and heard back from Brian James, vice president for engineering and manufacturing, who requested the Change White Paper she offered in her email. Her response is as follows:

> Dear Brian,
>
> Thanks for your response. It's one of our most requested papers. You will find it attached here. Please let me know

if you need anything else and I'll follow up with you in a
few days.

Thanks,
Jennifer

She also sent the following email each to John, CEO, and
Mary, CFO:

Dear Joe and Mary,
Cc: Brian

FYI, Brian has reached out to us for some information.
If you also would like a copy of our white paper that Brian
requested, "Next Year's Changes and Risks," please let
me know.
 If there are any questions you need addressed, feel free
to reach out.

Thanks,
Jennifer

She also heard from Bill Jarvis, the manufacturing manager
who is interested in looking at some machine tools. He's requested some brochures, and she sent him some right away and
placed a phone call to him, with no answer yet.

CHAPTER 4

By Territory, by Industry, by Persona

Salespeople make more calls in the last month of the quarter than the first two. The success rate of those last-minute calls are lower than the previous two months combined.

Conversion Rates reveal that at least 50 percent of your prospects in your Stage 1 are not a good fit for what you sell. Why waste time? Learn to qualify and disqualify early.

YOU NOW UNDERSTAND how people buy and why an ATL or BTL would need to change. It's time to get ready to outbound.

Hold on for a second. If you want to be effective in your outbounding efforts, you have to do a little planning. Not a ton of planning that will take you away from your job, but some planning so you have a much better chance for success. Call it the 80/20 homework plan—20 percent of the time to get 80 percent of the results.

IT DOESN'T MATTER

Sales territories can be divided in three ways.

1. Geographic—defining an individual or group by a geographic boundary.
2. Industry—a person's or group's goal is based on a certain industry, like auto, pharmaceutical, technology, and the like. This allows industry knowledge to be a strength in the sales process.
3. Product—many companies divide their sales goals by product line. This has potential for multiple salespeople calling on one account, but many companies have product-centric quotas based on their go-to-market strategy.

There are even some subgroups under these headings.

1. Persona—aligning sales efforts by business title or business functions, for example, CEO, CMO, CIO, Marketing, IT, HR, Sales.
2. Market potential—looking at the market through annual revenue of the company, number of employees, or potential spend. Examples would include SMB, Mid-Market, Commercial, and Enterprise.
3. Existing vs new—subdividing the market into clients who currently do business with you, and ones who

don't. A classic hunter/farmer mentality—hunt for
new logos or expand the logos you currently have.

4. Product vs service—this subdivision is popular when a
company goes to market with a product and the
services part is really a separate sale. Many companies
try to attach services to an initial sale, while many
companies do not.

There are a few more popular ones, but however you are
aligned, unless you have total, free reign, which some companies
have, you will have a definable territory.

That said, here are some homework variables you want to consider before you start with your outbounding efforts.

▶ Go where you are strong.
▶ Go where the money is.
▶ Go where the problems are.
▶ Go where decisions are quick—energy.

GO WHERE YOU ARE STRONG

Your company has certain markets in which it does well. You have
certain types of titles in which you have done well. Capitalize on
your strengths. Make a list of them. Ask some questions to get
some answers.

▶ In what market have we done well?
▶ Where is our competition the weakest?
▶ Is there a strong geographic market in which we
do well?
▶ Is there product we replace well?

▶ Are there users in a geographic area that we can leverage?

▶ Do our customers have different divisions or partners you can leverage?

▶ Is there a current event on which we can capitalize?

▶ Does our product lend itself well to a certain time of year?

Also look at personal strengths that could impact success.

▶ Knowledge of an industry
▶ Knowledge of a group of people
▶ Current customer base from a previous job
▶ Friends and business contacts
▶ Research skills
▶ Business acumen skills
▶ Ability to build rapport

Your knowledge and strengths, as well as the company's strengths and successes, will give you confidence in how you approach a target market and will increase your chance of success.

GO WHERE THE MONEY IS

Certain industries have more money to spend than others. For example, the software industry has gross margins higher than 90 percent and should be looked at as an area to start exploring. Other industries work on a 3 to 5 percent gross margin, and their ability to easily change from one process to another is not as easy.

Line of business (LOB) executives usually control the money. They need to develop an annual budget and work within it.

They can move money around to pay for things during the year. This "rob Peter to pay Paul" capability comes in handy for non-budgeted items.

Production, engineering, manufacturing, product, marketing, and sales are usually LOB areas that have budget money to spend since they can easily affect top-line revenue, which is usually top of mind with the executive suite.

Staff functions that serve the LOB, like IT, HR, and finance, are usually a longer sales cycle, since they need the support of the LOB to make a change. The exception is IT, where it may be making the decision for a LOB and get funding from it.

When doing your research, look to where that industry or that company is growing and spending money.

Growth is a key word, since most companies want to grow and will tell their stakeholders where growth is coming from. Is it from new logos (market share), is it from a new product line, a geographic expansion? Find the stated growth areas and start your outbounding efforts in these areas, too. The chance to get a conversation going is usually higher since the need for growth requires changes.

GO WHERE THE PROBLEMS ARE

In their simplest form, companies have initiatives and goals. If their stated goals were easy to obtain, they wouldn't want to talk to you. What is keeping the ATL executive from obtaining a goal? Usually problems. What problems, challenges, gaps, snags, glitches, and difficulties are preventing the ATL executives from obtaining their quarterly or annual goals?

You will see in later chapters that these gaps are major areas of concerns to ATL executives, and they would love help in getting them resolved. That's where you will be coming in.

GO WHERE DECISIONS ARE QUICK—ENERGY

It never shocks me when I see how long companies' sales cycles are. How do companies accept these drawn-out sales cycles?

> Our sales cycle is initial contact, then discovery, then a presentation, followed by a demonstration.
>
> We typically have to go to a proof of concept (POC) or some sort of trial, then a POC review, followed by a final discussion on options and pricing, which then is delivered in a final proposal. Then it's on to legal and purchasing, and finally the order.

Really? That's acceptable? You have to prospect where the energy is, and energy is usually with an ATL. Tap into this energy and your outbounding efforts will pay off big time. Not only will you get a better outbounding response rate, but you will get a better lead and a quicker sale.

THE LAW OF SALES CYCLE LENGTH AND ENERGY

I did some work for a company a few years back, and we started the conversation with a discussion of sales cycle length and average sales price (ASP).

It turned out that they had a typical sales price of $60,000 and an average sales cycle length of 135 days.

I told them that's impossible, since taking 135 days to sell $60,000 is really not cost effective. I don't know if I said *cost effective*, I think I might have said *stupid*, or something else to that effect.

They explained to me that I did not understand their market. I explained to them they didn't understand business. To go on, we discussed a "real-life scenario."

Mary, the vice president of digital marketing, just came back from a bad executive off-site. The meeting was to finalize plans for the upcoming fiscal year, and she took a beating. She was chartered to grow the online business segment by 60 percent last year, and it looks like it will come in about 35 percent. That translates to a $20 million revenue loss. Not insignificant.

"I know the results aren't what we want, but we got off to a slow start, had some initial web traffic problems, and then the payment option vendor we chose never delivered and we had to switch. Based on all the unforeseen chaos, I think we did OK, but we are in great shape to deliver the expected 65 percent growth targets for next year as we have been discussing," Mary said to the executive team.

Grudgingly, the executive team has given her a short rope, and she must deliver on the new goals, no questions asked.

Mary is in her office now, a few days after the executive meeting, talking to Bob, her manager of e-commerce.

"Bob, we really did not deliver last year. I know we had some problems, but why were the numbers so low? Was it our hit rate, churn, cart abandon rate, what?" Mary asked Bob at a lunch meeting.

"Mary, I can make some guesses, but if we really want to know, we need to do some testing. If you want, I can buy some testing software, and we can really see what went right and what went wrong."

"Testing, yeah, that sounds good. How much, Bob?"

"Oh, $60,000 to $80,000 should do it."

"Man, that sounds steep, but we need this, so go ahead. I'll get you the budget by the end of the week."

OK, so Bob gets his budget, takes 135 days (that's four and a half months) to select a vendor, sixty days to run a test, thirty days to get the results and make a recommendation. That's more than seven months. News flash—in six months, before she can get the testing results and make changes, Mary's fired.

An ATL buy business decision (buy cycle) would be, let's say, 30 percent of that 65 percent growth (call it $20 million for fun). It is a risk, with Mary telling Bob, "Bob, make a decision on a vendor in two weeks, start testing, and get me results by the end of the month. I can't wait."

Well, there's a 135-day sales cycle that just went to thirty days, and $60,000 to help a roughly $20 million problem is not a tough decision, period. Go where there is energy to help you get better responses to your outbounding efforts.

THE SALES MATRIX AND POWERHOUR

Finally, the subject of time management always comes up when you talk about outbounding. As I explained in my previous book *Knock Your Socks Off Prospecting*, there is a good time management tool that is easy to implement called the ProActive Sales Matrix.

This tool will give you a clearer understanding of the way you are spending your time today and make it far more obvious how you can find time to prospect among the really important opportunities. You only have so much time—you need to spend it wisely and not avoid the hard stuff, which is what you probably do.

To begin, let's start with a typical sales forecast, time-management scale that ranks prospects as A, B, or C. This is the way a salesperson usually forecasts, with percentages of getting the deal.

A = Current hot prospects. These are accounts you're banking on. Usually a 90 percent factor is assigned to these prospects. (This means the salesperson is 90 percent sure of the deal coming in.)

B = Medium prospects. These are works in progress, somewhere in the sales funnel. A 60 to 70 percent factor is usually assigned to them.

C = Lukewarm prospects. More than likely these prospects have recently been identified, they are just starting the sales cycle, or they are "hope and a prayer" prospects. These accounts usually get a factor of 10 to 40 percent.

These weighted averages are OK, and can get the sales manager in trouble if he or she believes them (more on that another day), but there is a lot more information available for you to use than just a one-dimensional, weighted guess.

To turn that forecast into a far more effective time-management tool, let's change the meaning of the letters a bit and add a second dimension to the A, B, and C ratings. The first dimension will represent history—what the prospect has done with you or your competition.

The second dimension will represent the potential for future activity on the account. To keep things specific and realistic, let's limit our projections of future activity to the next ninety to 120 days.

A = Sales greater than $100,000

B = Sales between $30,000 and $100,000

C = Sales less than $30,000

Thus, instead of an A prospect, your prospect might be AA. The first "A" refers to past activity on the account, the second to projected future activity.

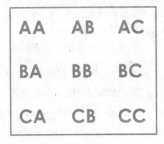

AA	AB	AC
BA	BB	BC
CA	CB	CC

So an AA account is one that has spent more than $100,000 with you in the past or currently (first "A") and has the potential in the next 90 to 120 days to spend more than $100,000 with you again (second "A"). If you assign BC status to a prospect, that means the account currently or in the past has spent between $30,000 and $100,000 with you and has the potential in the next 90 to 120 days to spend less than $30,000 (see Figure 4.1).

Now you know two valuable things: *Why* it is worthwhile to devote some time to prospecting, and *where* we should be spending most of that time. You have identified your Red Zone. Obviously, you need to provide for the care and feeding of the major accounts you've already got, but for outbounding purposes, don't focus too much on the first letter in a prospect's status equation, unless your job is just to outbound for upsell opportunities. For

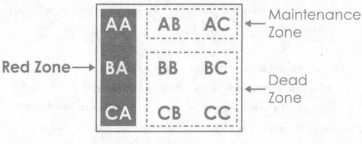

Figure 4.1

regular outbounding efforts, the really important prospects are the ones with an A or B as the *second* letter.

You'll never get a shot at a major prospect if you're just going after the small, easy ones. Salespeople miss great prospecting opportunities every day simply because they have developed habits that keep them focused on the wrong opportunities and therefore are looking in the wrong direction.

They also are nervous (read lack confidence) going after potentially important opportunities, since fear of blowing it keeps gnawing at their brain. You should look at this ProActive Sales Matrix to give you the logical proof you may need to overcome your fears.

The Dead Zone—this is where salespeople typically spend 50 to 70 percent of their time going after easy accounts that they have some contact with or have done some business with. It should be 10 to 25 percent.

The Dead Zone is filled with customers calling in with problems or questions, with very little potential for additional business in the near future. It's also filled with prospects who will never spend a lot of money with you. Tire kickers. Hobbyists. You justify it because it's the low-hanging fruit.

•　•　•

> ▶ Law of Low-Hanging Fruit

My uncle had an orange tree where he lived in Florida. When we visited, we would always attack that orange tree for fresh oranges. The low-hanging fruit was the easiest to get. Didn't need a ladder or a step. Just went up and picked them.

Well, after the low-hanging fruit was gone, we then had to work to get the fruit at the top of the tree. Guess what? Those oranges were better. They got more sun and were much better tasting. Bottom line, the fruit is better at the top of the tree.

The 80/20 rule applies here: Approximately 80 percent of your customers generate 20 percent of your revenue—and 80 percent of your problems! There are actually some customers in this zone you may wish would give their business to the competition. Outbound to these people sparingly. Yes, it's easier, but not really fruitful unless your timing is right.

The Maintenance Zone—also called the Comfort Zone. Here we find the customers and prospects we consider important. They are the bread and butter of our territory. They have spent a lot of money with us in the past and have the potential to spend more.

Currently, however, their budgets or buying windows do not justify a great deal of our prospecting time. Yes, there is business to be had, but in the short term (the next 90 to 120 days), you can find better uses for your precious outbounding time and resources.

The Red Zone—Those really hot, big opportunities are out there, and there are prospects that have the potential to spend a lot of money with you. If you want that money, you need to invest some prospecting time. So, here is where you do most of your homework and invest most of your prospecting energy.

Red Zone accounts should be clearly identified, and 10 to 30 percent of your *total* time should be proactively spent here. Concentrate especially on accounts at the BA and CA levels, or on trying to move accounts into a BA or CA status. Why? Because you already know the AA accounts. Chances are it's the BA and CA prospects that are crying out for more of your time, effort, and outbounding skills.

An example should explain the matrix more clearly.

> Jennie wanted to proactively look at her account base and figure out where she should be spending her time. She determined an A account should be one where the revenue is $100,000 or above, B accounts are from $50,000 to $100,000, and C accounts are from $10,000 to $50,000. Any accounts below $10,000, she kept off the forecast.
>
> She also said her second digit, time, was for a sixty-day window.
>
> By using the ProActive Sales Matrix, Jennie determined where she needed to spend her time as well what was needed to go after some accounts in the Red Zone. She had too many potential leads and was not working smartly.

Do you spend a lot of your time going after little fish when you could spend more time going after whales? Now you know what you can stop doing in order to make more time for prospecting.

Be proactive and make sure you are spending at least 20 percent of your time in the Red Zone and less than 50 percent of your time in the Dead Zone. Look forward, not backward. In the next thirty days, look and see where you are spending your time. Use your company and personal strengths to help qualify where to spend time, and apply the matrix.

As for how to spend that outbounding time wisely, the ProActive Sales Matrix logically gives you an objective view of what you are doing now and what you need to do to be successful in the future.

POWERHOUR

What's the first thing you do every morning when you start work?

You look at your email, check your voice mail, get yourself organized, and by the time you look at the clock, it's 11:00 a.m., and you wonder where your morning went. Maybe your New Year's resolution was to get hold of your time and use it, as opposed to it using you. And maybe you've made the same vow every New Year since 2015.

Your outbounding efforts will become far more effective when you turn outbounding into a behavior and not a "whenever you have time" type of activity. How can you do that? Welcome to PowerHour.

PowerHour is a one-hour-a-day, five-hours-a-week tool that you set aside to focus on a particular activity—in this case, outbounding. The activity thus becomes a normal part of your day rather than something you'll get around to when you aren't busy. Tragic truth: The day will never come when you aren't busy.

Look at PowerHour like a workout in the morning, and reward yourself for completing it. Order that special cup of coffee. Treat yourself to something you enjoy. Make a deal with yourself that if you complete five honest PowerHours in a week, you'll go online and buy that special something you've had your eye on. Devise a reward structure that works for you, and do yourself a favor. You'll have earned it.

There are three types of PowerHours:

1. For the occasional outbounder
2. For the medium outbounder
3. For the heavy outbounder

The Occasional Outbounder—PowerHour for the occasional Outbounder is a great tool. You will be able to do all of your account homework and cold calling within the five-hours-a-week time frame. Typically, you should start by devoting 50 percent of those five hours to homework and 50 percent to execution. The more you prospect, the less time you should need to spend doing homework, so your ratio will rise to something like 70/30 in favor of actual outbounding.

The Medium Outbounder—The medium Outbounder may require two PowerHours per day. Devote one hour to homework and one to outreach (or spend half of each PowerHour on each of those two activities). Whatever schedule you devise, stick to it. Try like crazy not to break the routine you set up for yourself.

The Heavy Outbounder—If your sales situation demands that you spend a majority of your time prospecting, try to do your "homework" PowerHours in short, fifteen-minute segments. This gives you time to get into a groove when you are outbounding, then do homework when you need a break. We think you'll find that you'll be more productive that way. Again, this should be a daily behavior, not just something you do every so often.

Don't forget that goal we talked about before. Focus on the Red Zone during your PowerHour times. Who is in the Red Zone, and whom can I get into the Red Zone with some work? That's where you'll find the best returns on your time investment. Before you know it, you'll be able to buy yourself ten special somethings.

THE STORY

Jennifer and Jerry met for coffee again a few weeks after their last meeting.

"How's it going, Jen? But first, have I got something to tell you," Jerry said. He was excited to tell Jennifer how he thinks he has this really good potential account on the hook. "Yep, this account is perfect for us. I heard back from their marketing manager, and she wants to have a presentation in a few weeks. Word on the street is they are gearing up to do more work next year, which means they will need more leads. Better yet, they are in a B2C market where we do really well. Jen, I'm telling you . . . Bingo!"

"That's great, Jerry. If you remember, you said you were going to get five leads. What's going on with your other outbounding effort?"

"Oh, it's going. You know, once you get a whale on the line, it's tough to keep fishing, but I'll get there. How about you? What's up?

"Well, I got a request from an ATL prospect for a white paper we are sending out, so that's good. I also sent out a status email to other executives in the company to keep it alive."

"What?" Jerry was floored. "You get an ATL prospect on the line, and you go over their head? What planet are you on? You are going to make that ATL buyer mad!"

"No, not over his head, just keeping as many people as I can in the loop so when it comes time for a decision, we are past the introduction stage and all the ATLs who need to be involved will be onboard. My AE's really like that I reach out to more than one ATL when I get a lead, especially an outbound one. Makes their job easier is what they tell me."

"Oh, good, but I really don't trust anyone but myself to make an ATL call. You never know how fast you can turn an ATL off by saying the wrong thing. I'm not trusting any of my SDRs to do that. I learned the hard way."

"To each their own, I guess." Jennifer exhaustingly blurted out what she was really thinking. "Anyway, I'm doing some research and I've targeted ten potential accounts I want to go after, and at least three have the potential to be in my Red Zone."

"Glad to see you're doing homework there, Jen. What's a Red Zone?"

"Thanks. That's what I call a targeted account that has the potential to be a really important deal for us. I'm trying not to just go for the small fish, but go after some important ones, too."

"Oh, that's a good idea. I just don't seem to have the opportunity to do all the homework that you are doing. You know, I have to bring in sales, too!" Jerry's now pretty proud of himself since he just got another shot at why AEs are so busy and more important than SDRs.

"We're all busy, Jerry, but I'm trying to be organized about it."

"Well, that's good. Let's see how my whale does against your homework. See you next week? Same time?"

"Yep, as long as you're buying, I can't afford to pass up a free coffee. Have a good day!"

PART 2

Getting to Work

With the background and customers viewpoint behind you, it's now time to get to work. How to prepare and organize so you can kill it.

CHAPTER 5

Preparation

More than 50 percent of inbound prospects want to see a demo on the first call. Fewer than 10 percent of outbound prospects want to see a demo on the first call. What's the difference?

THE PREPARATION TOPIC for outbounding is always a half-full-half-empty debate. Too much preparation, and you never make any calls, too little preparation, and you don't come across as creditable or confident. What's the answer? Stay tuned.

PREPARATION 101— SEQUENCING AND CADENCES

Putting together a sequence of events or touches to form a cadence is a critical step in outbounding. Without this tool, you'll be doing one offs and wondering why no one wants to get back to you. The InsideSales.com (now Xant) sequencing model is a good place to start. They look at the five elements of a cadence and make sure they are well thought out and aligned with each other to make a great sequence for the target outbound audience.

The elements of a great sequence are:

1. Attempts
2. Media
3. Duration
4. Spacing
5. Content

Attempts

This will be the number of attempts a salesperson will use to contact a prospect. The number usually suggested is between five and ten attempts. Most salespeople usually make two to three attempts, thus the wide gap between expectations and success.

Salespeople usually think that five to ten attempts are too many, and they think they will be seen as spamming or stalking their prospect. The reality is that the prospect is busy, and if you use all the elements of a good sequence correctly, the prospect ends up admiring your hard work and persistence. We have examples of twenty-plus touch sequences that are very effective.

To add one more brick to this pile, if you are going to outbound, and try two to three attempts in a two-week window, you should expect less than a 10 percent response. You are much better off doing fewer targets and more attempts in that two-week window than trying to shotgun your prospecting efforts. Leave the shotguns to marketing. You need to focus and use a rifle.

Media

There are many forms of media—the best ones are email, voice mail, social media, social video, and direct mail. Don't laugh at direct mail. In a B2B sale, it really can be effective, upward of a 95 percent open rate!

Oh, and unless you know the person or have had some interaction with that person before, texting is still not an accepted outbounding tool. In some industries, some cultures, if you are on your fourth or fifth touch, it is common, but other than that it is still rare.

Duration

There are three elements to duration you want to pay attention to—length, market, and calendar.

> Length—the length, measured in days, of an outbound cadence will depend on your target and market of course. The government market typically takes longer than the SMB market and so on. Use a bit of common sense in your duration length equations.

That said, in a B2B world, a two-week cadence seems to work about the best. It's a controllable time frame and it can be a very effective. Why? Read on.

Spacing

The data on spacing covers two areas:

1. It seems like the accepted standard right now is a two- to three-day spacing in between touches. If a touch gap

is longer than two or three days, you will lose the attention of the buyer. (Frequency illusion effect coming up.)

2. A two- to four-week gap between cadences is also acceptable. If the "buyer's window" is not open during your first two-week cadence, then give it a rest for two to four weeks. This should allow the buyer's window to open again, the prospects' "fire" that took all their focus has probably passed, and they may be more receptive to things that could help them to change and meet goals.

Content

The content of the touches is obviously very important. Since this is where you will be doing most of your work, and it's what the prospect really sees, there needs to be some basic rules:

1. It's Not About the Dog. For years we have told salespeople to not talk about themselves in the initial contact as much as possible. Everyone agrees, but no one ever listens, so we developed a metaphor called "It's Not About the Dog." No woofing, no barking in these initial contacts. It distracts from your message. See below.

Hi, John,

Joey Young passed me your info and *I would love to connect with you briefly to discuss our current collaboration tools for your company.*

Not sure if you're familiar with us, but we are the number one customer-rated video communication solution in the

market and are changing the way organizations meet and
collaborate.

Do you have a couple minutes today or tomorrow to chat?

(The italicized parts, which we did, are about the dog.) The
more you can get the prospect's attention and the less you talk
about yourself, the better, although we find it's easier said than
done. Save talking about you for later in the sale.

2. Write to the persona. Write to an ATL differently than
    a BTL. Here's some general ideas.

BTL Value	ATL Value
Easy to use	Advances a corporate initiative
Has the right features	Saves time
Great support	Lowers risk
Is within the budget	Solves a problem on an initiative
Integrates with what I am working with	Gives a competitive advantage
Makes me look good	Adds value to company brand

Search on the web "What keeps a CXO awake at night in
20XX." You will be surprised how much there is available to you

and in the CXO's vocabulary. Also, do a search on conferences and their topics. Every year, Gartner tries to get CIOs together for a conference. Look at the agenda. If Gartner says these are topics CIOs should be interested in, well, they probably should be some topics you should use as well.

3.   One Swipe. With so many messages being opened on mobile devices, the one-swipe rule applies. Send the email to yourself and look at it on your mobile device. If it takes more than one swipe to read the message, it's too long.

Woof – too much too!

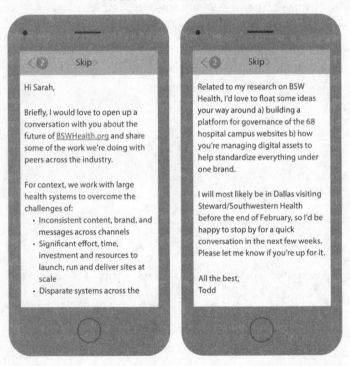

Better

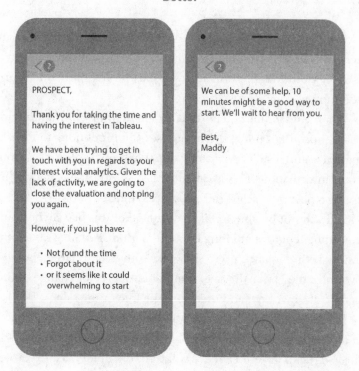

There are more ideas in regards to content later on in the book, but for starters, these are good ones.

CONTROL THE CADENCE AND SEQUENCING

Bottom line, test and control the cadence and the sequencing. The more media channels you use, the better. You will get a better response from using social, email, and voice mail than you will by just using email. Expand and contract the touches based on who you are trying to reach. The more you test, the better you will get.

FREQUENCY ILLUSION

Did you know our brains are really wired to look for patterns? It helps makes sense out of the daily chaos. By being consistent in a two-week window, the prospect will start paying more and more attention to your efforts.

When your brain detects that an element of information appears more than once, the brain uses the repetitions to form a sequence and dismiss everything else that is not repeating as irrelevant information. This is called a bias. So now there is a way to create a positive bias in your prospect's mind . . . wow!

You will not be able to take advantage of this bias if your outbounding length is not long enough, period. Two weeks is a minimum, with guidance up to six weeks if the sale is large enough. Typically, the larger the sale, the higher degree of change, more people are involved, and therefore the longer the sale.

Frequency illusion is a great way to get the prospect's attention and to separate you from the noise. However, more than a two- or three-day gap in your cadence will reset the timer back to zero.

Example of an 8-Touch 10-day Sequence

WHAT TO DO:	Day 1	Day 2	Day 3	Day 4	Day 5	WKND
EM - Email					EM2	
VM - Voice Mail			VM1			
SM - Social Media	SM1					
DM - Direct Mail						
IP - In Person						
TX - Text						
PC - Personal Call			PC1			
VID - 1 Min. Video						

WHAT TO DO:	WKND	Day 6	Day 7	Day 8	Day 9	Day 10
EM - Email					EM3	
VM - Voice Mail						VM3
SM - Social Media	SM2					
DM - Direct Mail						
IP - In Person						
TX - Text						
PC - Personal Call			PC2			PC3
VID - 1 Min. Video						

• • •

Example of a 14-Touch 20-day Sequence

WHAT TO DO:	Day 1	Day 2	Day 3	Day 4	Day 5	WKND
EM - Email			EM1		EM2	
VM - Voice Mail	VM1					
SM - Social Media	SM1					
DM - Direct Mail						
IP - In Person						
TX - Text						
PC - Personal Call	PC1					
VID - 1 Min. Video						

WHAT TO DO:	WKND	Day 6	Day 7	Day 8	Day 9	Day 10
EM - Email						
VM - Voice Mail					VM2	
SM - Social Media		SM2				
DM - Direct Mail						
IP - In Person						
TX - Text						
PC - Personal Call					PC2	
VID - 1 Min. Video						

WHAT TO DO:	WKND	Day 11	Day 12	Day 13	Day 14	Day 15
EM - Email		EM3				
VM - Voice Mail						VM3
SM - Social Media						
DM - Direct Mail						
IP - In Person						
TX - Text						
PC - Personal Call						PC3
VID - 1 Min. Video						
WHAT TO DO:	WKND	Day 16	Day 17	Day 18	Day 19	Day 20
EM - Email						EM5
VM - Voice Mail				VM4		
SM - Social Media						
DM - Direct Mail						
IP - In Person						
TX - Text						
PC - Personal Call				PC4		
VID - 1 Min. Video						

No, this is not spamming. It's hustling. You have something the prospect may need, so why would you waste your time or theirs?

When I wrote my first book, *ProActive Sales Management*, I sent it into the publisher pretty proud of my work. In a few days, I received an email saying they really liked the book, but I started quite a few my sentences with "I think" and "I believe."

They informed me I'm writing like I talk, and not how readers want to read. I had to drop the "I think" and "I believe," since the reader would not take this as my passion for the subject, but as arrogance.

Cadences are the same way. You think you're spamming; yet the receiver likes your hustle. If anyone thinks he or she is being spammed, you'll hear about it . . . and most of the time. when they tell you to stop, it's your messaging . . . woof.

SUMMARY

Develop your own sequence. Start easy, something you feel you can accomplish. Try the eight-touch, ten-day sequence for ten outbound prospects. That will get you going. When you reach one, drop it and add another, so you always have ten sequences going. This should take no more than one to two hours a day to work, so have at it, and adjust as your results and goals dictate.

Just so you know, twenty-five ten-day sequences are not unheard of, and really are some best practices that are out there right now. Two hours per day . . . go figure.

THE STORY

Both Jennifer and Jerry had tons of news. Jennifer went first. "Man, what a good week. I heard back from not only my initial ATL, but the CFO as well. Seems like they are looking to grow their business with a new product line by $10 million this year and $20 million next year, and they don't have the capacity to do all the additional work. I've been talking to their manufacturing manager, and it seems we may have a machine that would be perfect for them, so we scoped out two new machining center platforms to get production under control. It should be a $100,000 to $200,000 order for my AE.

"Additionally, I was told that they need these new machines by June, which is within our ship dates. They did mention they believe that launching their new product is being held up by the ability to manufacture. I need to follow up on this."

Jennifer was on a roll after her call with Royal. "We were on a video call and most of the time they were talking among themselves. I just listened and actually heard them saying that they would love to get the machines up and running by May. The CFO even mentioned she could see an additional $1 to $2 million in revenue if they could get these tools earlier than normal. The manufacturing VP told her that was impossible, so that ended the conversation right there, but I'm still going to check in and see what we can do."

"Wow," Jerry said. "Seems like you have had a few good calls."

"Yeah, then I called the CFO back and told her I was checking into an earlier delivery, and she said to let her know as soon as we can. The RFP came out a week ago, and it states June delivery, so who knows what's going to happen."

"Well, I'm doing pretty well myself," Jerry bragged. "I got a thirty-day trial for a new system in a company. They won't start using a new system until the second quarter next year they told me, but that's OK, I can start next year off with a bang. But to tell you the truth, the trial will be over this year, and if I can make them a sweet deal and get it in this year, that makes my year. You never know about these things."

"Congrats to you, Jerry. How are your other efforts going to fill the funnel? You know that's what we are talking about here, not getting an order."

"Yeah, I know, I know, but if I can get this one in by the end of the year, I'm set. I'll get around to outbounding in a few weeks when they start their trial. What have you been doing for outbounding?"

"Well, I've got ten cadences going, and I think three will pan out, and possibly two of the three will be this year's business."

"Cadence, what's a cadence? If you want to outbound, you look at your territory, ask yourself where is the opportunity, and you hit it. Don't take no for an answer, either."

"Jerry, how old-school of you."

"Well, tried and true works, and I'll get to outbounding for a few more prospects in a few weeks, too. I'll have the time then."

"Oh, man, I'm late, gotta run," Jennifer blurted out as she started running for the door. "Same time next week?"

CHAPTER 6

Prep and Numbers

The use of collaborative words has a positive impact on your outbound messages. Using "we" instead of "I" increases success rates by 35 percent.

INSIDE PREP

The homework and preparation you do for a current customer and a new logo should be about the same. Try not to allow yourself to do surface homework on an account just because they do business with you and "they know us." Most likely, your relationship is with a BTL, and that person does not have the information needed to expand your business inside the account.

Set Goals

There is no real secret to setting goals. It's something you must do, and you need to write them down. All this "I have them in my head" stuff doesn't work.

Goals should be looked at every day. It's how you start your day off, making sure you work on important stuff rather than urgent stuff.

- Important stuff—Things that you do that will help you make your quota.
- Urgent stuff—Things that you do that keep you busy, but really do not help you make your numbers. The stuff you do that keeps you from doing the hard part of your job, filling the top of the funnel.

KNOW YOUR NUMBERS

There are three sets of numbers you want to track.

1. What is going on to fill the funnel?
2. What's in the funnel?
3. What are my success ratios?

What Is Going to Fill the Funnel?

The initial work you do to fill the funnel every day is probably the most important. It is about quantity and quality.

Quantity

- Number of outbounds per day
- Number of cadences active
- Number of ATLs vs BTLs in funnel
- Number of cadences that reached conclusion
- Quantity of potentials to start a cadence

With the typical salesperson having a two-touch-then-give-up approach (which is unbelievable, since it takes me more than two attempts to get my kids to call me back), the ability for you to succeed with a two-touch cadence is really low.

An 8/10-touch ten-day, or 10/12-touch fifteen-day, cadence will put you in the driver's seat. You must, however, keep track and be diligent in your outbounding efforts. You can't skip a day or just give up midway (see PowerHour). If you think like a customer, you know they are really busy, and the fact they don't get back to you right away is not necessarily an implication of they don't want to talk to you, they're busy. Keep trying.

You goal for the number of cadences is up to your needs. Ten is a good number to start, but how much funnel coverage do you have and need relative to your quota?

Coverage is a very subjective term, but we can try to define it based on stages and qualified numbers. Our definition of a qualified account is one that is in at least Stage 2, and the ATL has been contacted, and their Solution Box B has been identified.

Example: You have a quarterly quota of $200,000, and you know you want 2X qualified coverage. (Many SDRs are goaled by deals closed, not just deals thrown over the wall. Use metrics that make sense to you.)

▸ If you have 50 percent coverage, so $100,000, you need ten to twenty cadences ongoing.
▸ If you have 100 percent coverage, so $200,000, you need five to ten cadences ongoing.
▸ If you have 200 percent coverage, so $400,000, you need five cadences ongoing.

Remember, cadences last for roughly two weeks, so the number of monthly cadences you start is double the above numbers.

Monthly cadences started:

▸ If you have 50 percent coverage, you need to start twenty to forty cadences in the month.
▸ If you have 100 percent coverage, you need to start ten to twenty cadences in the month.
▸ If you have 200 percent coverage, you need to start ten cadences in the month, or two to three per week.

Quality

It has to be quality over quantity nowadays, and here are some basic quality metrics.

Quality of ATL activity

ATL activity is trying to get to an ATL, getting to an ATL, or getting direction from an ATL. The directional email to an ATL is a good tool to use when outbounding. That's the one where you ask the email for directions.

> Mr. Smith,
>
> After doing some research, it may be beneficial for our companies to talk. Who in your organization would be chartered to look at AI in the sales automation space, specifically how AI is shortening sales cycles and increasing average sales price?
>
> If this is a current project or at least on your radar, whom should we start our conversation with?
>
> Thanks in advance.

The successful attempts made to the ATL will directly relate to the quality of the attempt. If you talk about Solution Box A all the time, talk about you, or talk about the dog, your success rate will be low to nonexistent. You need to make sure the ATL contacts are short, concise, focused on them, and have an ask.

The general rules for outbounding quality include:

1. It's all about them.
2. Use "we" and "you," never "I."
3. Make it about them, their title, or their company/industry.
4. Call to action within a 24- to 48-hour window.

Quality of the Cadence

Cadence quality follows a few rules.

1. Keep the message short, no more than 100 to 120 words. Yes, you read that right.
2. No more than two to three days between touches.
3. Think of a cadence as a sound bite. A little bit of info with a lot of touches. Not just one hope-and-pray email dump (woof).
4. The more communication channels, the better.
5. Each touch should follow a message pattern or a story. Referencing past touches and announcing future touches has proven to be very successful.

Quality of the Outbound Source (Referrals Are the Best)

You need to get the prospect's interest, and referrals are the best way to get someone's attention. LinkedIn is, of course, a good source for a B2B sale. The bio has some good information, but there are two great areas outside of the bio you should also investigate.

1. Of course, the mutual connections part—knowing someone they know, or even knowing someone who works at a company that you may have in common, is a great lead source.
2. The skills and endorsements area. This is a great area.

Skills & Endorsements   Add a new skill

New Business Development · 99+

Tyson Gaylord, Transformation Shaper and 99+ connections
have given endorsements for this skill

Sales Management · 99+

 Endorsed by **Tim Farmer and 2 others who are highly skilled at this**

Coaching · 97

Zach Baughan and 96 connections have given endorsements for this skill

Show more ⌄

Look up what individuals or what individuals in certain companies have recommended the person you are researching. In these three areas—New Business Development, Sales Management, and Coaching—there are almost 300-plus potential contacts you could reference. Even if you don't know anyone, if you find three people in one company, even if you don't know those people, you still can send an email saying, "I see that you have three people in the

ABC company who have recommended you on your LinkedIn profile. We do work with that company. Small world," or something like that. It works. Familiarity is one step closer to rapport.

Besides using LinkedIn, you need to get out there. Trade shows, conferences, industry events, just show up at the breakfast and cocktail hour and plan to meet ten individuals. The more you expand your network, the better off you will be.

Obviously, your health club, tennis club, golf club are great sources. Don't forget your own company. Send an email out to people in your company saying you want to contact an individual or a company. It is amazing to me how many salespeople, less than 32 percent, ever ask for a referral. You might be surprised what a small world it really is.

Of course, news articles, blogs, and posts about the company or about the person are good, timely ways to get in touch with an ATL prospect.

What's in the Funnel?

Sales funnel management is always a fun topic. A sales funnel is full with A, B, C prospects. What should be in the outbounding funnel?

The earlier you score your outbound leads, the better chance you have of a working funnel. There are a ton of lead scoring systems out there. Just Google it and you'll get a host of ideas.

The best ones add and subtract scores, typically on a scale from 0 to 100. Also, look at the conversion rates by stage to see how well the prospect moves through the sale, and don't forget to measure days in each stage, a key metric for energy in a deal.

A typical scoring system:

▶ 10 points for an inbound BTL lead
▶ 25 points of an inbound ATL lead

- 10 points for a call longer than five minutes
- Add 20 points for an outbound lead connect
- Add 20 points for an agreed homework assignment
- Subtract 10 points if they do not want to do a homework assignment
- Add 10 points if they can recommend others for you to talk to
- Add 10 points if they agree to a next and next/next step
- Subtract 10 points if they don't (Tire kicking)
- Add 10 points for overcoming an objection
- Add 10 points if next step is within a three-day window
- Add 20 points if they discuss I-Date (Implementation Date)

Usually, anything scoring higher than 80 is a good lead, 50 is a warm lead, and below 50 is a "needs work." Play with this and tailor for your situation. It's a good way to take some subjectivity out of the lead-generation process and stay focused on give/gets, not just the emotion of the thrill of "I've got one."

A good funnel management scoring system will change, based on who you are calling, dollar value of the sale, the market you are in. A $100/month service should take a lot less time to get in and out of a funnel than a $10,000/month service.

Figure 6.1 shows another example of a scoring system. For this company, with 38 total possible points, anything above 20 is sent to an AE.

OUTBOUNDING QUALIFY SCORECARD		
SOLUTION FIT		
	1 or 2	Our solution can definitely do the job
	2 or 3	You have identified at least one train, and have QC
	3 or 4	ATL has agreed with GAP Analysis
	2 or 3	BTL has a decision criteria that we can meet
	2 or 3	You have multiple trains and multiple GAPS
Possible 15	Total	
VALUE TO US		
	2 or 3	If you get this business, both you and the prospect will make money
	2 or 3	There is good upsell potential
	2 or 3	This prospect is in our target and will be a good logo
	2 or 3	You have a solid relationship with ATL and BTL
Possible 12	Total	
BUDGET AVAILABILITY		
	2 or 3	Budget is allocated or ATL knows where they can get the funds
	2 or 3	Decision Process and Budget Process are Defined
	4 or 5	There is a sense of Urgency to invest now
Possible 11	Total	
Possible 38	Grand Total	

Figure 6.1

What Are Some Good Success Ratios?

Here are some personal numbers.

1. It takes four to six attempts to contact a warm lead.
2. It takes six to ten attempts to contact a cold lead.
3. If you do not have an ATL discussion after Stage 2, the deal is less than 50/50.
4. The more media you use in your sequence, the higher the probability of success.
5. You need to have 4x to 5x of funnel activity in Stages 1 and 2. In essence, if your monthly quota averages out to three deals, you need to have twelve to fifteen deals in the first two stages of your pipeline.
6. Same ratios go for cadences.

Develop a Team

The saying goes you should never water ski alone, never snow ski alone, and you get a better workout at the gym if you buddy-up. Same with outbounding. Inside or outside of work. Your manager, peers and others that you should trust should support you in your goals. Friends too.

Create a team that will challenge your homework. Create a team that will help develop and modify your cadences and your messaging in those cadences.

Develop a team of people you can share your goals with and the probability you will achieve your goals will massively increase.

Public Shouting/Declaring of Goals

The more you publicly announce your goals and progress, the harder you will work on them. Have a leaderboard, a progress board, or a milestone report showing successes. Get more and more people supporting your efforts, and you will be surprised how much others really want to help you. Ask, and watch what happens.

OUTSIDE PREP

You are ready to start prospecting. You need to get your outside sources aligned.

Social

In a B2B setting, most people think of LinkedIn as the authority. It has revolutionized outbound prospecting. There are more social sites than LinkedIn, like Dynamic Signal, EveryoneSocial, Dun and Bradstreet, Facelift BBT, Grapevine6, Hootsuite, PostBeyond, Sociabble, Glib, Slack, and Thought Horizon. Not to mention Twitter, Instagram, and Facebook. Needless to say, your LinkedIn page better be in top shape. Also, leave out the pictures of you in a tux/formal, your family, the dog, the chickens, the garden, and so on. Your customer wants to deal with quality, not "a great parent or farmer."

The market has quite a few tools for you to use, and with advances in AI, expect this to grow. However, the commitment to using social is very small. Forrester Research found in a recent study, only 25 percent of respondents said they consistently equip sellers with social engagement tools and an even smaller portion—only 8 percent—have optimized such practices. Looks like you will have to do some of the heavy lifting yourself.

The goal here is to have a strategy. Where can you get the most leads, not the most followers or connections.

THE STORY

Jennifer was really happy. She just flipped a highly qualified lead over to her AE and really believes she has a new solid lead. She actually started to add some more prospects to her funnel as well and was in research mode. She believes she has a process down and is going to keep refining it.

Jerry was late, but filled with news. "Seems like my prospect just issued an RFP, and I think it's perfect for us. I called the marketing manager and asked her if she wants to see a demo, and she said they are not in too much of a rush right now, and will select vendors they want to have demos with right after the first of the year. This is looking good for next year. Well, I guess I need to fill up that funnel again so I can try to get one more in this year."

Well, you know the story. Jennifer has a process and a cadence system down and will continue to prosper because of her outbound process. She will be successful because she has the numbers and activities to make it happen.

Jerry has no clue that his prospect will be making an early decision based on the commitment the CMO has made to get a system up as early as possible. He's still just talking to the BTL and having the BTL as his "champion." He believes he is in the driver's seat.

When the marketing ATL tells the marketing BTL the new time commitments, Jerry will be playing catch up. He's not in control of the sale, and you know how that usually ends up.

The moral of this story: Work the process, period.

CHAPTER 7

What Works

The average person deletes 48 percent of the emails he or she receives every day in just five minutes.

IT'S NOW TIME to get on to messaging. Getting your outbound strategy going is important, of course. The messaging is more important, however, than how you are delivering the message. Here are some key thoughts to adhere to.

ALL ABOUT THEM

Go to a party this weekend and don't talk about yourself. Just have people talk to you about themselves. You will find it fascinating how much people like to talk about themselves.

It just feels good talking about yourself. It really does. For most people, our own thoughts and experiences are our favorite things to think and talk about. Research shows that people spend 60 percent of conversations talking about themselves—and goes to 80 percent when using social media platforms such as Twitter or Facebook. Amazing.

Why do people, especially salespeople, spend the majority of their time talking about themselves and their solutions? It's because it feels good.

Research at Harvard has shown an increase in neural activity in areas of the brain associated with motivation and reward when people are talking about themselves. It's the same area that we get gratification from happy experiences, good food, and positive rewards.

Talking about yourself and your point of view, your features and benefits in a sales situation, is enjoyable and makes salespeople talk more about themselves and their products, features, and benefits, regardless of the need to talk about the customer's problems and how to resolve them.

Bottom line: Talking about yourself, your products, and their benefits is intrinsically rewarding. The research also showed it was rewarding even if *no one was actively listening*. From a social standpoint, just the idea of posting information about us and our accomplishments, in text or pictures, makes us proud. We love talking about our favorite topic—us.

The bottom line for salespeople is this: Many salespeople have had great success just pitching features and benefits. Since they enjoyed doing it, they have convinced themselves that it's the right thing to do. My reply, *woof.* (It's not about the dog.)

It is incredible in client emails, how much they mention themselves. Here is an example of a real one, names changed, of course.

Dear Mr. Smith,

I would like to introduce myself. I'm Skip Miller, a senior account manager for XYZ. We are a leading marketing services company that gives business owners the best marketing tools they can get. We have:

- Insightful, forward-thinking social marketing solutions
- Great support
- Solutions to your problems

I would like to review with you a report on the marketplace. It will show you what we are doing, and you will be able to see how what we do is actionable and can provide you with the information and solutions you are looking for.

At XYZ, we are committed to providing you with the solutions you need today. If you could please return this email, I'll be happy to send you the free "Landscape for the Upcoming Year" report.

Looking forward to hearing from you.

Ok, let's go.

1. I would like to introduce myself. I'm Skip Miller, a senior account manager for XYZ—I didn't ask for an introduction. Instant delete.
2. We are a leading marketing services company—Who cares? What does it mean for me?
3. We have insightful, forward-thinking social marketing solutions, great support, and solutions to your problems—You don't know what my problems are, so how can you have solutions?
4. I'll be happy to send you the free "Landscape for the Upcoming Year" report—Is this relevant to my business? My current business challenges?

Unfortunately, this was a perfect example of what not to do. Here's another.

> Hi, Paul,
>
> I recently read in the *Tribune* about your partnership with XYZ Biomedical to combine technologies in an effort to better monitor glucose levels in diabetics and *I was inspired to reach out to you.*
>
> *At our company, we work with global brands like XXXX and focus on "Digital Transformation" and business outcomes in IT and Line of Business.*
>
> More than 65 percent of the Fortune 500 companies currently *use our data.* We have more than a thousand analysts worldwide providing global, regional, and local expertise on technology and industry trends as well as written deal review and contract analysis.
>
> *Who is the best person for me to speak with at ABC to introduce our company to yours?*
>
> Thank You.

The italicized words (my edits) are all about his company and what they can do. You have to make the prospecting outreach all about them. Hint—no one is going to read these, let alone take action. Just make these messages more about them. Here's a quick change to the first one. It's far from perfect, but it does switch the emphasis from "I" to "them."

> Dear Mr. Smith,
>
> As you assess next year, CMOs like you are asking real world questions like:

- What lead generation issues have I *not* thought of as I adjust my annual plans?
- How can I get faster results *without* investing in unproven marketing ideas?
- How can I *decrease my risk* for the rest of the year in lead generation?

There are no crystal balls, of course, but many CMOs are looking at the end of this year and are seeing some gaps in their strategy. Let's talk and see if we can address some of those risks.

Regards.

P.S. If you could please reply to this email, I'll send you a recent report on what lead-generation ideas CMOs are investing in that really work.

Here's the second one:

Hi, Paul,

Interesting to see in the *Tribune* about your partnership with XYZ Biomedical to combine technologies in an effort to better monitor glucose levels in diabetics. Fascinating.

The challenges for next year will be in "Digital Transformation" and business outcomes in IT and Line of Business. Right up your alley.

It's possible the outcomes you are looking to implement next year, we may know something about. More than 65 percent of the Fortune 500 companies, including many in your industry, currently leverage our data.

> Who is the best person for me to speak with at ABC to
> introduce our company to yours?
>
> Thank you.

Again, neither one is perfect, but they focus on the customer and potential outcomes they may be trying to get.

ATLS AND BTLS ARE DIFFERENT

It's been defined what ATLs and BTLs do. A general definition is ATLs have the ability to "rob Peter to pay Paul," in other words, they can move money around in their purview. ATLs can take assigned money from one project and reassign it to another.

BTLs get "budget" money. It's what they can spend on specific projects. Anything more than what's been budgeted needs to get approval from an ATL.

What are the titles and duties of some typical ATLs? I found this on the web and thought it summed it up nicely.

CEO—The chief executive officer, or executive director, is the person in charge of the management and administrative direction of the organization. The CEO is at the top of the chain. In the majority of cases, the CEO is also the founder and drives the purpose, vision, and mission of the company. Responsible for connecting the business with the market, having the final say in budgeting, investment decisions, and directing the company's strategies so that it achieves its objectives.

COO—The chief operating officer is in charge of the day-to-day administration and operation of the business. The COO reports directly to the chief executive officer (CEO) and is considered his/her right hand. In some corporations, the COO is also known as the executive vice president of operations.

CMO—The chief marketing officer is responsible for marketing activities, which typically include sales lead generation, product development, advertising, market research and customer service.

CFO—The chief financial officer, also known as the financial director, is in charge of the economic and financial planning of the company. Deciding when and where to invest, assessing risks, all in order to increase the value of the company. Contributes financial knowledge, accounting, and provides a general and analytical look at the business.

CIO—The chief information officer looks after the systems of the company that are related to information technology at the process level and from the point of view of planning. The CIO analyzes the benefits new technologies can offer, identifies which ones are more interesting to the company, and evaluates its operation. The CIO focuses on improving the efficiency of internal processes in order to ensure effective communication and keep the organization functioning smoothly.

CTO—The chief technology officer oversees the development and correct operation of information systems from the point of view of execution. Generally responsible for the technical teams and to implement new strategies to improve the final product. A similar role to the CIO position, since in some companies they share tasks. The key difference is that a CIO focuses on information systems (communication workflow), with the aim of increasing efficiency, while a CTO is responsible for the technological strategy aimed at improving the final product.

CCO—The chief communications officer is responsible for managing corporate reputation, contacting the media and developing Branding strategies. Media relationship to guaranty the brand awareness, and positive imaging. The CCO aims to have positive feedback and favorable from clients.

CSO—The chief sales officer, sometimes called the CRO (chief revenue officer), is responsible for sales from all channels, be it direct, partner, white label, or channels. Sales will get measured on revenue, and some cases profit. Making sure all product lines and geographies meet revenue expectations is a common goal, along with setting the next year's goals, territories, and compensation. The CSO also is responsible for sales operations and sales enablement.

BTLs usually work for an ATL, and it's their job to make sure the projects and initiatives that the ATL are working toward are met.

One more difference between ATLs and BTLs is value. The BTL value proposition is to make sure whatever they buy is used correctly. They are the ones who are going to be using whatever you are selling them, and their decision criteria is going to be aligned with what you and your competitors' stuff can do.

An ATL has a different value criteria than a BTL, and we call the ATL value proposition VAT.

VAT—VALUE ACTION TIME

I am on a mission to destroy the term *decision maker* since for most B2B deals, there are two, the BTL and the ATL decision makers as we described before.

> ▶ Two Value Propositions

The BTL and ATL value propositions are very different. Here's an example you might relate to.

During the holidays, most people have their relatives and other family members and friends over. Typically, there are so many people at the big dinner table, not everyone can fit. So, the host breaks up the dinner into two tables, the kids table and the adult table.

The kids love it because they don't have to speak adult, and the adults love it because they don't have to speak kid talk. Two different value propositions.

ATL is going to see things differently than a BTL, and when outbounding, you really have to know what is important to an ATL, and that would be VAT.

1. The transaction must add value to both parties.
2. It must be actionable. Some action must take place on both parts.

This action must happen by a certain time, or within a certain time frame. "Soon," "ASAP," "in the next few months," and "by yesterday" are not specific times, so they do not count.

"Time" actually figures into the VAT equation in more ways than one, as we'll see. Let's look at the factors individually.

•　•　•

Value

Value, in the prospect's mind, has five elements.

Return on Investment (ROI)—Customers are greedy. They want their money back. As a matter of fact, they want more than their money back. They want two or three times their money back. Prospects look at the financial transaction first to see if it makes sense for them to get involved.

Time—Prospects will always pay for time. Increase up-time, decrease downtime, reduce overtime, speed up time to market— time really is money, and if you can tell a persuasive story about how you'll save them time, prospects will listen.

Risk—At the ATL level, it is all about risk. Everything is about risk. Make their decision more sure or less risky (help make them smarter or less stupid), and you will turn a prospect into a customer. Typical risks include:

- Competitive risks
- Pricing risks
- Geographic risks
- Political risks
- Investment risks
- Product risks
- Delivery risks
- People risks
- Manufacturing risks
- Engineering risks
- Integration risks
- Basic risks of the business
- Legal risks

Risk is the major reason an ATL will or will not make a decision. Why do you buy life insurance, health insurance, car insurance, and homeowner's insurance? To reduce your risk.

Motivational Direction—Understanding prospects' motivation helps you create value. Motivational direction can be summarized as a desire that pushes us either *toward* something or *away* from something. We call this tool *toward* and *away*, toward pleasure or away from pain.

Are your prospects running away from a pain, fear, or uncertainty? Or are they running toward a vision, a strategy, a goal? If they aren't doing one or the other, what do they need you for? You can find out their motivation by asking "why?" questions. Why is the prospect taking the time to speak to you? Usually you'll get answers like these:

▸ My old one is broken (away).
▸ I want a new style (toward).
▸ I like the new features (toward).
▸ The one I have just doesn't do what I need to do anymore (away).

Motivational direction discussions should mostly be put in an away mode, since 80 percent of the world are away prospects. They are motivated for away reasons. If it's not broke, they will not spend time fixing it, period.

Brand—Brand creates value. Shoppers pay more for Rolex, Polo, Tory Burch, and Mercedes. Business prospects pay more for Intel, Apple, Tumi, and Monte Blanc, since brands create pull. What can your brand do for the prospect? Better yet, what can your brand do for their brand so they can sell more widgets?

Brand can also be internal. "By buying this widget, my employees will know I care for them, and maybe that will lead to getting more top-level candidates to hire, since we seem to have a major shortage in this area (away)."

Value is *not* about spewing all the reasons you bring value to the table.

No one cares about your value proposition or your UVP (Unique Value Proposition). What they care about is *their* value proposition. Help them in *their* value, and you have struck gold.

The only way to do that is to ask them what is important about ROI, time, risk, and brand, not by telling them about your ROI, time, risk, and brand.

Action

"Yes, I can see your point, and I agree it would make me more money. I am just not in a position to do anything right now."

For value to be realized, there must be some action you and the prospect can take to make it happen. Just to agree there is value and then agree that nothing can be done to achieve it does nobody any good.

No action, no value. No value, no energy. Therefore, no action, no qualified lead. Create a sense of urgency, usually using time or risk, and then request that the prospect do something to move the deal closer to fruition.

Time is really a good one. You can use deadlines, goals, or commitments to your advantage, and these time commitments do not necessarily have to be the customer's, they can be general commitments like end of the quarter or start of a buying season.

Some possible commitments you can use could be:

▸ End of quarter financial goals
▸ End of year goals
▸ Holidays

- Vacations
- Weather events, like ski season
- Midyear goal adjustments
- Start or end of a promotion
- Trade show announcement
- Social media promotion

Businesses always have some events or commitments going on. Use time forward and backward to help create action and urgency.

- "Well, John, what is happening over the next few months that, if you had a different solution than what you have now, things might be different?"
- "Faiza, if you had a solution to this issue three months ago, what would be different?"
- "Ron, imagine you had this project up and running three months earlier, what would you be doing in addition to just solving this problem?"

By using time as a questioning format, you can invoke some sense of urgency.

Time

We said that, to meet the Value Criteria, the action in a transaction must take place within a specific time frame. We also said that time is one of the building blocks of value—customers will pay you to save them time. (That's why FedEx makes the big money.)

●　　●　　●

Time Traveling

To take things a step further, time comes in three tenses: past, present, and future. We call this time traveling. Your prospect's values in any situation will have to do with one of those tenses.

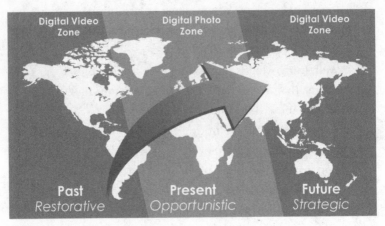

The prospect's motivation is either:

▸ Restorative—The prospect merely wants to restore something to the way it was in the past: "I really just want to get back to where we were before we missed that product deadline."

▸ Opportunistic—The motivation is to take advantage of a present opportunity: "Well, since I'm buying these tires today, getting the oil changed will save me another trip, and it's on sale."

▸ Strategic—Forward-looking. The prospect wants to invest in something now, so it will pay dividends in the future: "If I make a decision on this today, I'll lay the ground work for next year three months earlier."

The secret to VAT is asking questions, not telling everyone with a deck of forty slides what you do and how good you are. ATLs live in the past and future. BTLs live in the present.

One more time. ATLs live in the past and future. You ask them a present question, and watch how fast they send you to the BTL decision makers, and good luck getting back to the ATL. You are not in their world.

Prepare questions based on your homework for the ATL in these areas, and you will get the prospect to start talking, since it is all about them, their favorite topic.

"Let's look at the next few months . . ."

"What happened three to six months ago that is causing you . . ."

"As you look at the next few quarters . . ."

Value, Action, and Time are what prospects care about. That's what you should be selling to. How do you do it in a cold call? By asking questions as soon as possible, and potentially combining the VAT areas.

▶ "What do you see as the biggest risks facing you and your company in the next few months?"
▶ "What are your current problems in getting your product to market? Do you see value in getting to market sooner? What about three months from now instead of your scheduled six?"

▶ "If you could save 20 percent of your inventory carrying cost over the next six months, would that be of value to you?"

These questions are a heck of a lot better than statements like:

▶ "We can save you time and money."
▶ "We have the best product on the market, and we can make you more money."
▶ "We have the right solution that everyone wants now."

Click. Dial tooooone.

Statements make you feel good and proud, but is not what the prospects want to hear yet.

Great salespeople aren't the ones with great answers and statements. They are the ones with great questions. That's how buyers create value. It's all about them.

CHAPTER 8

Daily/Weekly Skills Scorecard

The most important thing about keeping score is knowing the game you are playing.

MOST COMPETITIVE PEOPLE always want to know the score. It's how they track their success. Without a scorecard, who really wants to play? Well first, you must determine the game you want to play.

All salespeople want to make quota. The sales quota game is the one salespeople play, because their company is measuring them by it. It's how they get paid, and how they keep or lose their job. The game of sales is usually based on quota.

Outbounding is another game. Yes, the results are more sales and more credit against quota, but to win at the outbounding game, you need to keep track of two elements: skills and activities.

If you hear someone tell you sales is a numbers game, tell them they are half right. To be successful at the game of outbounding, it's about skills and activities.

SKILLS SCORE

To name a few of the skills needed.

- Research Skills
- Organization Skills—System Skills
- Overcoming Fears
- Listening Skills
- Value Skills
- Multimedia Skills
- Attention-Getting Skills
- ATL/BTL Skills
- Product Knowledge
- Time Management Skills

Skill	My Current Score	Score by EOM	New Score
Research Skills	5	6	
Organization Skills—System Skills	4	6	
Overcoming Fears	5	5	
Listening Skills	6	7	
Value Skills	8	8	
Multimedia Skills	7	7	
Attention-Getting Skills	4	5	

Skill (continued)	My Current Score	Score by EOM	New Score
ATL/BTL Skills	6	9	
Product Knowledge	5	8	
Time Management Skills	7	7	

How would you rank yourself on a scale of 1 to 10 on these skills? Look at this example. Here, the salespeople rank themselves and what they want to be by the end of the month (EOM).

This is a good scorecard for the rep to remember to get better at their skills, they need to "sharpen the saw."

Research Skills

How well can you systematically do research? Do you have a process? Here's a typical one.

Research the Company

Go to the company website. Really understand its mission and what problems it's trying to solve. What changes does it have to make and why? Assuming it's solving problems, ask yourself, What is it not doing? What are competitors doing better? What are their customers demanding that they will have to change to help them?

Assume problems like customer churn and developing next level products. Read the bios of the senior executives and do a LinkedIn on the ones who matter to you.

Quickly search for any recent third-party publications that discuss the company? Look for a company blog. Go over their news announcements and look for changes they have made, since changes always cause problems.

Has the company just published an article or white paper on a topic? Look where their industry research firm ranks them and possible discusses their strengths and weaknesses.

Research the People

Do a LinkedIn search on its executives that matter to you. How long have they been with the company? How long in that title? Where did they go to school? Who do you know in their LinkedIn profile that you know? What companies do you know that they might know?

Try to do more ATL homework than BTL homework so you can start your outbounding efforts at the right level to begin with.

Be in the Customer Chair

A good way to really understand your customer is to try being in their shoes or be in the customer chair. What is the company trying to do in the next twelve months? Increase revenue? Launch a new product? Cut costs? Partner with another firm? Be in their chair and ask questions.

"How can I get more profitable?"

"What are the roadblocks to a successful product launch?"

"How can I cut costs and still meet revenue goals?"

If you are targeting a group of people in the marketing department, then add that information.

"How can I get more leads and not increase cost?"

"What are the roadblocks to a successful new product launch?"

"How can I cut costs in marketing efforts and still meet revenue goals?"

Looking at the prospect as helping them solve an identified problem will give you more of an interactive initial discussion with the prospect than pushing them to a demo.

Organization Skills—System Skills

Daily Outbounding—Prospecting must be a habit, or it will always be something that you have to get to but never do. The best sales-people I know who are 200 percent of their quarterly quota are always prospecting, and do it in a highly organized manner.

Usually an hour a day, and that's it. You cannot find anything more important in a sales role that this habit.

Write a Script—Yes, write it down. Without it, you will get lost and possible lose control of the conversation to the prospect. Here is a good outline of a script. It lets you be proactive and not just winging it.

1. Introduce yourself and then pause—let them process and maybe even ask, "Yes, what's this about . . ." it starts a conversation.
2. State why you are calling—"The purpose of my call . . ." gets right to the point. Note: An alternative step here is to ask, "Is this a bad time?" It's a question, it makes them think, and if they say "Yes, it's a bad time," you

can work together to find a good time. This is a much better question than asking, "Is this a good time?" (Thanks, Quinn, for the tip.)

3. Get ready for objection number one—Ask for clarification or relate to a story.
4. Tell me more—Prepare a few questions in advance for your persona.
5. Next Step—Always have some options ready for a next step, don't ask the prospect what they see as a next step . . . there goes control.

You can search on the web and get hundreds of scripts, some good and most bad. The good ones allow you to be you, and not some robot. If you want to get them to laugh up front, and that's your style, go for it. It you want to ask permission first because you know how to get past that objection, go for it. The best scripts need to be tailored for your style.

Focus on the Next Step

See above. If you have a direction you would want this call or email to go, state it. Most people do not want to think of next steps, since they really are not experts at buying. Possible next steps include:

▶ Spend fifteen minutes discussing.
▶ Who in your organization should I be talking to?
▶ Where should I go to get more information?
▶ Set up a quick ten-minute presentation/demo.
▶ Send information with follow-up date and action.

Be intentional and directional with your script. It will keep you on course.

Plan for Objections

The usual objections we hear on a prospecting call center around:

- ▶ Time
- ▶ Money
- ▶ Just Looking
- ▶ Needs Approval
- ▶ Indecision

There are numerous ways to address objections. Both email or on the phone, this should be planned for in your script. What is the usual top three or four objections you usually hear, and what are good comebacks. Plan for it.

Work the Cadences

Great salespeople really work their cadences. They have it down and work their schedule. You cannot get behind on a cadence, since you will lose you prospects interest and almost have to start over.

Overcoming Fears

Everyone has certain fears. Napoleon Hill was a genius in describing what he called the fears of man.

The fears he identified were fear of death, old age, loss of love, ill health, criticism, and poverty. Fears really do drive behavior in a positive or negative way.

If you expand his top-two fears with fear of the unknown and fear of failure, you can really see where salespeople fail at outbounding. Most salespeople hate rejection and feel if they get too

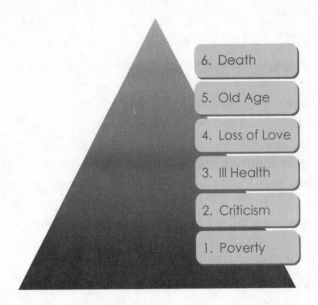

much rejection, they are not doing their job and may get fired. These fears stop a good salesperson form prospecting, especially the ones who have made a good life just following on inbound leads and now have to go outbound. Many are scared to death, and by just identifying their fears and learning how to overcome them, they can change this fear into a skill.

Listening Skills

You may find this data interesting:

- More than one out of two respondents indicated that, in a recent transaction, vendors clearly misunderstood their needs and pitched their products.
- 40 percent of prospective vendors simply failed to answer their questions.

▶ 42 percent said that the process would go more quickly if vendors stopped providing irrelevant information.

▶ 50 percent said that lack of technical/sales skills on the sales team "wasted their time."

▶ 45 percent reported that the sales team provided incorrect information. (Source: IDC)

Listening is a learned skill set. You can increase and improve your listening skills. First, some general rules around listening:

Ask Questions, Then Provide Benefits

Before you want to give a benefit of your product or service, ask a question.

"So, Ted, let me get this right, you think that if you could lower cost in your go-to-market strategy by 10 to 15 percent, that would be of interest to you?"

This is better than,

"So, Ted, my company has many customers who have lowered their go-to-market costs by 10 to 15 percent" (yep, woof).

The first one gets the prospect involved, the second just throws a benefit at the prospect and hopes he or she agree or wants to talk about it. Involvement in the first, spectator in the second.

Talk Less

You know you should but you can't help it, you are on a roll. It just comes out and it's now ten minutes since you started and you finally have come up for air. Not working.

A tip here is ask three questions before responding. Even if you have to use your fingers to do so (kinesthetic anchor). It really works and will make sure the client talks more than you. A good rule is 60 percent them 40 percent you at a minimum.

Involve the Customer

Always. Ask questions, use their name, get their opinion, give them a choice. Much better than show and tell.

No Interrupting

Let them finish their thought. If you interrupt someone, what you are really saying is what you have to say is more important than what they're saying. Is this really what you want to communicate?

Value Skills

Time and time again we hear salespeople state a value of their product or service which has no value to the customer. Years ago, I listened to a salesperson pitch their product.

"And to let you know, Boeing considers us a very valuable product."

Well I'm sure the salesperson was really proud that Boeing was using their product, probably a great reference too, but the prospect he was speaking to made gardening shears. Don't see many of those on a 787. True story. Make sure you have an idea of the customer value proposition, rather than yours.

The ATL and BTL value propositions have already been defined. The skill set here is speaking the right language to the right person, not just learning both value propositions.

Multimedia Skills

The research here is definitive. The more media types you use in prospecting, the higher the response rate. Social, email, mail, phone, and in-person skills should be evaluated here.

Attention-Getting Skills

In outbounding, you have a very short time to get and hold someone's attention. Recent research shows that the attention span of an individual has gone from thirteen seconds a few years ago to now eight seconds. Goldfish have an attention span of nine seconds, just saying. Also, when you are online, you have three to five seconds to capture or lose someone's attention. Attention getting is a skill set that can be learned.

ATL/BTL Skills

The features and benefits and questions you ask an ATL and a BTL are different. Good salespeople have skills in both these areas, not just selling skills.

Product Knowledge

This is the easy one that most salespeople feel they need help in, but it's usually the least important of them all. Customers buy for their reasons and any in-depth discussion in this area will drive the salesperson to a BTL and get ignored by the ATL.

• • •

Time Management Skills

The best outbounding salespeople use the clock to their advantage. They have a daily plan, down to the hour, and they work the plan.

Track Your Time

Where does all the time go? Most salespeople are unaware of the habits that kill their overall productivity.

Track specific tasks. You can do it in SFDC. Keep a goal of specific tasks that need to get done, and then track what you did. You'll see some patterns and you'll be quite surprised at how much time you have wasted.

Go Backward

People who set goals and monitor their progress are 25 percent more efficient those who don't. Set the goal and work backward by month/week/day to achieve it.

Working backward allows the numbers to be real, and gives you a pathway to meet the goals every step of the way, not just state for instance a quarterly goal, and then put it in a drawer until a week before the quarter end.`

"I will accomplish this goal by the end of the quarter. To do that, I need to be at this level by the end of month two. So, by the end of month one, I need to be here. That means I need to do this every week of the first month."

Having goals increases motivation and achievement. The more specific the goal, with a number, the greater the likelihood of success. A goal without a number and a time frame is a wish.

Grouping

Grouping tasks together leads to greater productivity. Block off a specific amount of time to make cold calls each day. Your cadences should be like clockwork. Designate an hour or two in the afternoon for certain types of outbounding activity like research or starting new cadences.

80/20 It

Eighty percent of your sales will come from 20 percent of your customers. That's true for a business, and very true for outbounding efforts. The sooner you can figure out the 20 percent, the better for you. You're either qualifying, or you're just talking.

One Thing at a Time

Multitasking actually slows you down. Your brain can't do two things at once. It's physically impossible. Prioritize your outbounding activities and focus on one thing at a time to maximize your success.

Plan Your Day Around Your Outbound Targets

If you're not emailing or calling potential customers when it's convenient for them, you're not effectively managing your day. Early and late are the best, and right before and after lunch as well.

The Swiss Cheese Approach

If it takes less than two minutes to do, just do it. If you have a few minutes, punching a hole in a big goal is far better than doing a whole bunch of little tasks that really don't matter. This is not a checklist completion exercise.

Activity Score

Activity scores can be in many different areas. Some of the most used are:

- Daily attempts made
- Numbers of cadences being run
- Number of ATL contacts/week
- Number of deals flipped to Decide

There are a ton more, but here is an example of a skills activity sheet that you should keep score with. If you are not keeping score and tracking progress, how do you know you are doing the things you need to do to get better? Oh, you'll know when the results change. Kinda late at that point, isn't it?

Track leading indicators, not trailing indictors. Now, let's add Activities to Skills in order to have a combined Skills and Activities Scorecard, as you can see in Figure 8.1. This will be your way to measure leading indicators that will affect results and contribute to your success. Use it.

Skill	My Current Score	Score by EOM	New Score
Research Skills	5	6	
Organization Skills—System Skills	4	6	
Overcoming Fears	5	5	
Listening Skills	6	7	

Skill (continued)	My Current Score	Score by EOM	New Score
Value Skills	8	8	
Multimedia Skills	7	7	
Attention Getting Skills	4	5	
ATL/BTL Skills	6	9	
Product Knowledge	5	8	
Time Management Skills	7	7	
Activities	My Current Score	Score by EOM	New Score
Number of Cadences Run	6	7	
Outbound Connects	5	5	
ATL Attempts	6	7	
Co Homework	7	7	
ATL Homework	8	8	
Meetings Set	7	7	
Deals Flipped	4	6	
Deals With Trains	5	6	
Deals Flipped With ATL Contact	8	8	
Percentage of Deals Flipped to Decide	7	8	
Percentage of Meetings Ghosted	6	8	

Figure 8.1

CHAPTER 9

Messaging: The Big Five

More than 60 percent of salespeople say that when they have something that works, like a presentation or certain questions, they don't change it. Scary thought.

HERE ARE THE Big Five reasons an outbound prospect would be interested in talking to you. Here are the golden tickets. These Big Five are areas for you to modify, personalize, and tailor to your audience. Yes, you will use some of the Big Five more often than others, and you will change each up rather than just sending out a blanket, nontailored email.

If you really want to know what will cause your prospect to have an initial interest, here are some ideas.

• • •

BIG #1—REFERRAL

After a positive experience, 83 percent of customers would be happy to provide a referral. But salespeople aren't asking—just 29 percent of customers end up giving a referral. —HubSpot.

There is no doubt that a referral is the number-one way to get your prospect to respond. People buy from people they like and trust, and an extension of that trust is a referral.

There are three types of referrals, Direct, Indirect, and Network.

Direct Referral

Ask for an introduction. Many salespeople see asking for assistance as a weakness. There seems to be a lot of Judgment on the referral front.

"Should I ask for a referral? I really don't want to put someone out."

"Asking for a referral is tricky. The person really needs to know me, and if I get a referral, I owe them something."

"I don't want to be pushy. If they want to refer business to me, they will."

A good time to ask for a referral is right after the customer signs the order. Don't wait for the product to ship and install or the service to be rendered. By then, you will be old news.

Right after they sign, send a thank-you letter to everyone you talked to at the account—not just the decision makers, but everyone. And they each get their own unique email, not one email to a ton of people; that's not cool. Individual thank-you notes are really effective.

> Mr. Smith,
>
> Just a quick note to say thank you for implementing the leading business tool on the planet, and if there is anything you need or if you have any questions, please feel free to reach out to me. It's been a pleasure to work with the ABC company team. You have a great team there.
>
> Additionally, if you know of any other people in marketing or other companies that could use our help or are having similar business issues that you had before you decided on XYZ, would you please forward this email to them? I appreciate the opportunity to help other people/ companies that you know.
>
> Thanks again,
Skip
>
> P.S., If Jim sent you this, I can be reached at skip@m3learning.com.

This email is pretty good, and it's not asking Mr. Smith to give up a name. It's asking him to forward the email to someone, and the fact that you made Mr. Smith look good in the first paragraph doesn't hurt.

Ask for Help

As you can see from the email above, asking for help is easier than asking for a referral. People love to help others, especially after they have just made a decision about you and your company. Oh, by the way, you did a ton of work to help them make that decision, and that decision is going to make them a ton of money.

One a Day

A good cadence for referrals is one a day. Targeting five per week might be easier and more manageable. Bottom line on these referrals, about one in ten actually end in a lead, and usually they are good leads since the people being referred know who you are and why they need to talk to you.

Leverage Your Contacts

Constantly ask people to add to your LinkedIn account. End your conversations with, "Oh, and by the way, we are always looking for good opportunities to help CMOs out (or whomever)."

Be specific about what you do, and you will get better quality referrals than just, "Hey, if you know of anybody . . . ."

Indirect Referral

If you work the system, it will work for you. Remember, referrals are the best way to get leads, so dedicating time here will be a wise move. Some of the best Indirect Referrals seem to be:

Past Customers

Stay in touch with past customers. Sincerely ask how they are doing and if there is anything you can do for them. Ask for referrals at the end, and be real, don't just say some nice canned words and then ask. Really do some homework. Here's a quick example.

Hey John,

Just saw your LinkedIn post. Nice. Thought the point about pipeline growth was right on. Just staying in touch. Hope you are well. Also, please remember, if you know anyone who can use our help, we are always around!

Take care. Have a good rest of the year,

Skip

Blog

Posting blogs is a great way to keep you in front of your customers. You also can reference these when you are outbounding or use them as attachments in your email. Start your own blog. The Blog Starter is a good reference on how to get started, and they recommend a five-step process.

1. Pick a blog name. Choose something descriptive.
2. Get your blog online. Register your blog and get hosting.
3. Customize your blog. Choose a free template and tweak it.
4. Write and publish your first post. The fun part!
5. Promote your blog. Get more people to read your blog.

Promote your blog to past customers, your LinkedIn connections, and even social groups that want something from you in order to join.

• • •

Interest Groups

Being a part of special interest groups is also a good way to keep your finger on the pulse of activity and contribute as an expert, or just get leads from the group. Almost all the social media companies offer a way to join and participate. You may be surprised how specific you can get, especially if you want to find groups that align with your territory or certain personas.

Network

Finally, make sure you network as often as you can. Many cities have local events with speakers and meet-and-greet sessions. Bring your business cards. Yes, they seem old-fashioned, but they are effective in getting your name out there when the situation arises.

If you go to a trade show or event, have a goal. The best salespeople I have seen at these events do some homework and set goals on the number of business cards they can pass out, and even certain people they want to meet. By the way, speakers at these events love hearing that they did a good job, and it puts you in a great situation to ask another question and network with the speaker. Happens to me all the time.

Bottom line, when looking for referrals, ask for what you want. Remember, this is a give-and-get society, so asking for leads when there is no benefit for the other side to help you is not a good strategy. The person with whom you are talking probably needs something as well. Ask: "What can I do for you? What's happening in the next few months where you might need some help?" It's always good to give something for every ask.

BIG #2—CURIOSITY

Make your prospect curious. Ask about themselves, their title, their competition, their industry, or their job. Curiosity is a great transfer-of-ownership vehicle and can get your prospect to think, which is usually the start of a question, which is the start of a conversation.

Psychologists at the University of California found that the human brain retains information better if we're curious. They also found the area of the brain that regulates pleasure and reward lights up when the participant's curiosity was piqued.

You have probably heard that only humans are worried and curious about reasons and causes for things. Animals are curious, but only we humans ask the question, "Why?" Additionally, there are two basic types of curiosity you choose from when outbounding.

Perceptual curiosity—This is when we see something that surprises or puzzles us or doesn't make sense with something we thought we knew. "I see what you are saying, but that doesn't make sense to me. I need to know more."

Examples:

- "Next year will not be like this year."
- "What you did last year will not help you next year."
- "You are looking at 20 percent growth, but did you know you can grow 50 percent with the same investments?"

Epistemic curiosity—the desire to learn new things. We are wired to expect rewards when we learn new things. Knowledge is power, and the more we know, the more powerful we feel. It's why when you get some news (gossip) about something that your friends probably don't know, you feel powerful for being the first one to share it.

Examples:

- "The new way to do things."
- "The XYZ company is doing something you should be doing."
- "Here's how your neighbor grew her investments by 50 percent."

Either one can be a powerful tool to get someone to call you back or take a call with you. Making someone curious, not by tricking that person but by using your homework to illuminate an area that would make your prospect pause, is an essential tool when you begin your cadences.

Attention

Creating curiosity captures the attention of your prospects without giving away too much information. This often makes them want more information, which is what you are trying to do.

- Trends you are missing.
- No leads? Here's why.
- Leaving money on the table with your customers?
- Market is booming. Are you onboard?

Help

Asking for help is a good way to get someone's attention. It has to be quick and easy.

Scientists have studied a phenomenon called "Helper's High." Helping someone actually releases endorphins that improve mood and help in self-esteem. People generally feel good, biologically, when they help someone. It is thought that helping someone feels better to the person who is helping than the one who asked for the help.

> ▸ **Some interesting scientific statistics:**
>
> - Helping others can help you live longer.
> - Altruism is contagious.
> - Helping others makes us happy.
> - Helping others lowers blood pressure.
> - Helping others promotes positive behaviors.
> - Helping others gives us a sense of purpose and satisfaction.

▸ "Can you please help me determine who in your organization. . . ."

▸ "Can you help me determine if this can be of help to your company?"

▸ "Would you mind helping me and introduce me to. . . ."

Asking for help seems easy, but for many people it is hard. Look at it this way: It's another way to help make your prospect curious and ask you for help.

Buyer's Calendar

Senior executives whose corporate calendar is the same as their fiscal calendar operate on quarters that can be predictive of their actions. Each quarter, what is top of mind for businesses is predictable.

In the first quarter, the ATLs are launching new initiatives, some of which are doing well and others are not. If you are selling something that can improve one of their new year launch initiatives—especially one that they are not feeling really good about—watch how fast a deal can move through the funnel. It's usually about the 80/20/80 rule.

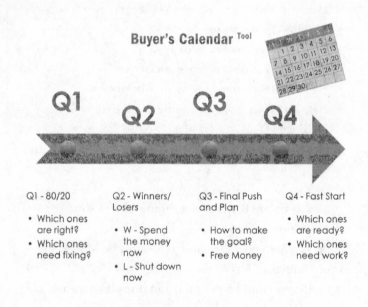

Buyer's Calendar Tool

Q1 **Q2** **Q3** **Q4**

Q1 - 80/20

- Which ones are right?
- Which ones need fixing?

Q2 - Winners/ Losers

- W - Spend the money now
- L - Shut down now

Q3 - Final Push and Plan

- How to make the goal?
- Free Money

Q4 - Fast Start

- Which ones are ready?
- Which ones need work?

ATL executives feel good on about 80 percent of the initiatives they started the year off with, but it's that 20 percent of goals that are not doing as planned that are causing 80 percent of the headaches. Help them identify and fix those 20 percent.

For the second quarter, decisions are being made on what initiatives to invest in and which ones to kill. They need to know by midyear, the end of the second quarter, so they can attack the second half of the year in full stride.

The end of the second quarter divides the business world into winners and losers. The initiatives that are going well (winners) will get extra resources and extra attention. These are the ones that are going to make the company's year. They will get their funding from the initiatives that are going to be scaled down or canceled (losers).

Winning initiatives get more resources and more funding and have to be spent fast, like in the next few weeks and months, if the newly acquired additional resources are going to have any effect on this year's results.

By the time the third quarter rolls around, the focus is aiming at last-minute adjustments for end-of-year success. The gaps for the year are being identified, and so initial thinking is being done on what needs to happen, what projects to ramp up, what things they can do to make the year a success and get their bonuses.

Finally, there's the fourth quarter, and there are two objectives at this time, which are:

1. Make the number for the year. Do whatever it takes so the executive team can make its bonus.
2. Get ready to launch the next year, and not waste the entire month of January doing so, thus falling behind.

When you start aligning your sales advances to the buyer's calendar, your probability of success has just increased.

Questions

Finally, use questions. Questions motivate the desire to answer and usually can start a conversation. By asking a question, you are engaging your prospect, making them think, and that is what you want when you are outbounding.

Did you know questions can hijack your brain? It's true. Watch.

What did you have for dinner last night?

This question actually hijacked your thought process. You just turned your brain on to think only of what you had for dinner last night. You didn't tell your brain to think about dinner, it just happened automatically.

Questions influence what we are doing right now and can also influence future behavior. That is a powerful weapon in the sales toolbox.

Questions trigger a mental reflex known as "instinctive elaboration." When a question is asked, it actually takes over the brain's thought process. And when your brain is thinking about the answer to a question, it can't really think about anything else. You are now in the front of your prospect's mind.

Neuroscience believes that the human brain can only think about one idea at a time. Your brain cannot multitask; it's impossible. When you ask a question, you force your prospects to consider *only* your question, and if it's a question about them, you get bonus points.

It really does feel weird to ask questions in an email or over the phone rather than give statements. Salespeople love statements. Why? People think their perspective or experience is important, and if the other person agrees or disagrees with a statement, since it is the seller's statement, the salesperson feels great to talk about the statement, since it is usually about them.

When asking a question, the unknown pops up, and salespeople usually don't feel good when they don't know something, so they stay away from questions. Additionally, since the questions are not about their products or services, they feel the prospect will not make the link.

"I can ask the prospect questions, but if they are not questions about us, what's the point?"

ATL buyers, over and over again, state what they hate about sales calls is more often than not that salespeople have *a solution looking for a problem,* rather than the other way around. If you want to see if you are good at questions and listening, play the question game.

▶ **The Question Game**

The game is played by two people. The object of the game is for the first player to ask a question to which the second player's response *must* be in the form of a question. Every question must be answered with a question until someone makes the mistake of answering with a statement. The game is lost by the player who failed to respond with a question.

You will find yourself really having to listen to the answers before you ask another question. Oh, and your responses must be directly related to the question you were asked.

You will find you will be answering a question very quickly without having heard what is really being asked. It is better to take the time to actually think about what the other person asked and then ask a question in return in order to gain clarity before answering. Good luck with this game, and notice how you feel when you are asked a question. If the question is about you, you'll feel good and want to answer. No statement, just questions.

BIG #3—THEM

The outbound message that says, "Yes, it's about you," is one of the most powerful ways of getting prospects to open your email or take your call. Personalization must be real and well thought out. Calling someone "Bill" when he really wants to be called William is not helpful, and it also should not come across as a template. People really do like seeing their name in lights.

- Janice, stop losing customers.
- Looking for some answers to next year, Justin?
- John Doe, happy with your e-commerce results?
- Coming to Dreamforce, Mary? Drop by our stall.

Be careful with all of them, because they can come across as a standard marketing automation template. You can make it about them, though, by using social information (saw your post on LinkedIn), by title (Most CMOs in California) or by industry (Many CIOs in the printing industry . . .)

BTW, the jury is still out on using Mr./Ms., first name only, or first and last name. The data is not that clear on what you should do, so the answer is to consider the industry and title you are sending to, not just what is your style. Some industries are more formal than others, and you should adapt your introductions to the prospect, not the other way around.

BIG #4—NUMBERS AND LISTS

Numbers and lists are among the most powerful tools that can be used in subject lines and blog posts. Why? Because they are effective. Using numbers in the subject line or body of an email attracts attention, as your people's brains are drawn to digits, which is why top-five or top-ten lists are so successful—lists are easier for our brains to process, and they create curiosity. They also hint at a possible quick read.

▸ Five steps to turn around your SEO
▸ Top three ways to stop wasting time
▸ Four reasons why you can't reach your prospects
▸ Three ways to stop losing customers

Use the digit 3, do not spell out the number three. It's the digit, not the number, that causes you to stop and think.

BIG #5—TIME TRAVEL—SELL OUTCOMES

Time traveling is a great tool to cause the prospect to contemplate. It uses the brain, and the brain loves to time travel. The brain loves to go back in time and remember, it goes forward in time and imagine. It loves to time travel and by using time traveling in your outbound messaging, you can actually begin the transfer of ownership of your solution.

Urgency

Using urgency in an outbounding messaging is a classic way to create concern. Most of us have a natural fear of being left behind, of missing out—that herd mentality is a survival instinct. (For example, "Only three seats left," "Only good for four more hours," etc.)

Additionally, combined with motivational direction, people respond better to the threat of losing (away) rather than to the promise of gaining (toward) so urgency can be a powerful messaging technique when used in your cadences.

- ▶ Only two weeks left to hit this quarter's goals.
- ▶ What would you redo if you could regarding your lead generation over the last six months?
- ▶ Last chance to grab this offer.
- ▶ If you could do something now that would prevent mistakes next quarter, would that be important?

These are your Big Five ways to get noticed and get a prospect involved. Stay within these guidelines and don't drift to what you want to do. Your show-up-and-throw-up tendencies will take over. Keep the Big Five in mind all the time.

CHAPTER 10

What Doesn't Work

Using the word or action "discount" decreases close rates by 17 percent. So why are you doing it?

YOU NOW HAVE a ton of good information on what type of content and messaging you should use in your outbounding efforts. Let's make sure you really understand what doesn't work. It's important, because as much as you understand what does work, some will always go back to their old habits and, folks, it just doesn't work.

Oh, yeah, what doesn't work? Here are the Big Five for what doesn't work.

#1 THE DOG

One more time: It's not about the dog! The less you say about yourself, your company, and your mission, the better in these early stages of trying to connect with the prospect.

#2 TOO LONG

Most outbounding messages are more than three hundred words. General rules: not more than three paragraphs, not more than three sentences per paragraph, and bullets work better than paragraphs.

Novels

You want to be complete and not miss anything of value when you are outbounding, but you need to think like a buyer. No novels. They look good, but no one is going to read them.

> Hi John,
>
> I saw your post of Google's comment: "Be a data-informed company. Smart people, not data, should be making your decisions." I also remember your comment about your company's interest in the AR/VR market.
> Our data shows:
> 2020 VR hardware grew 132.4 percent at 10 million units sold. By 2023, it will be 52 million units.
> AR Hardware—exponential growth with 190 percent CAGR from 2020-2024.
> How do you plan to capture the opportunities in this market?
> We have the data, analysis, and insight to help you leverage this explosive opportunity.
> Does noon on Monday, September 20, or between 1:00 and 4:00 p.m. on Tuesday, September 28, work for you for a brief call to discuss how we can help you make your business decisions?

Here are just a couple of examples:

Impact of AR/VR on adjacent markets (smartphones, tablets, PCs, game consoles, and wearables)

Five-year forecast for purpose-built AR/VR hardware, associated software, services

Survey: What do consumers want from AR/VR? What are the early adopter demographics and pricing expectations?

Consumer AR/VR application deep dives: gaming, therapy/rehabilitation, and virtual experiences in travel and education

Thank you for your consideration. If those times don't work for a call, please let me know and we will work around your schedule.

Best regards.

OK, some interesting observations:

1. This is 212 words. No one is going to read it. Data shows your outbound messaging has to be 120 words or fewer. Yep, 120 words or fewer.
2. This is educating an ATL. Not a good idea, period. It's not what they care about.
3. It's all about the dog. Way too much woofing.
4. You should assume this is going to be opened on a mobile device. Want to see what that looks like? See below, and this is not even the entire email. You have one swipe, that's it. More than one swipe, and it will be deleted.

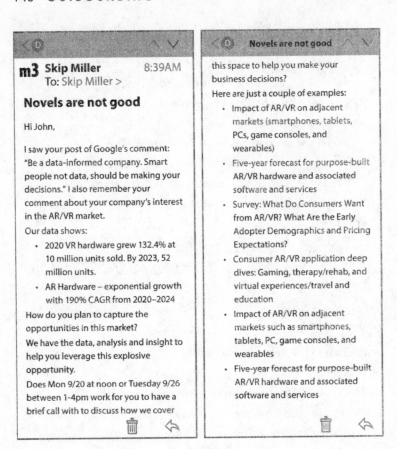

m3 Skip Miller   8:39AM
To: Skip Miller >

Novels are not good

Hi John,

I saw your post of Google's comment: "Be a data-informed company. Smart people not data, should be making your decisions." I also remember your comment about your company's interest in the AR/VR market.

Our data shows:

- 2020 VR hardware grew 132.4% at 10 million units sold. By 2023, 52 million units.
- AR Hardware – exponential growth with 190% CAGR from 2020–2024

How do you plan to capture the opportunities in this market?

We have the data, analysis and insight to help you leverage this explosive opportunity.

Does Mon 9/20 at noon or Tuesday 9/26 between 1-4pm work for you to have a brief call with to discuss how we cover

Novels are not good

this space to help you make your business decisions?

Here are just a couple of examples:

- Impact of AR/VR on adjacent markets (smartphones, tablets, PCs, game consoles, and wearables)
- Five-year forecast for purpose-built AR/VR hardware and associated software and services
- Survey: What Do Consumers Want from AR/VR? What Are the Early Adopter Demographics and Pricing Expectations?
- Consumer AR/VR application deep dives: Gaming, therapy/rehab, and virtual experiences/travel and education
- Impact of AR/VR on adjacent markets such as smartphones, tablets, PC, game consoles, and wearables
- Five-year forecast for purpose-built AR/VR hardware and associated software and services

#3 EDUCATE VS VALIDATE

The purpose of your outbounding efforts is to have a discussion with a prospect to determine if there is a need that can be addressed. During the buyer's process, he or she will have to be educated and validated. These are two unique steps for buyers, so make sure you are doing one or the other, not both.

A general rule: ATL buyers rarely want to be educated. They typically want to be validated about the outcomes their investment of time and effort will bring. What does not work is trying to educate an ATL buyer on who you are and what you do, not yet. Validate, don't educate when prospecting to an ATL.

> Mr. Smith, what my company does . . . is education

> Mr. Smith, if you need to lower costs and reduce customer churn . . . is validation

Proof Points

You need to get your prospect's attention, so offering proof points right now on why you are so good without establishing a need is like offering a tennis player all the reasons why you are a great golf club manufacturer. You need to zero in on the gap, not just throw out who you are.

Over the Wall

There are better ways than just throwing stuff over the wall and hoping for results, like an invitation to podcast, or the "I will be in your area" pitch. Sending stuff over the wall, like white papers and links when the prospect has not asked for them, doesn't work as well as when prospects reply back and say, "Please send it to me."

Many marketing folks will disagree. They send links and attachments out all the time.

Well, the data is clear:

1. Links and attachments have a tough time getting past firewalls and usually end up in the spam filter. Marketing counts it successful if they don't get a bounce back. Ha.

2. You didn't do a good enough job in the communication, the voice mail, or the email to create sufficient curiosity to make the prospect want to see it. By just throwing it over the wall, you think that will do it? Really?

3. If you are throwing stuff over the wall early in your cadence, you are really focusing your efforts on you, and not on your customer. Woof.

Free

I always love the free angle. Yes, people love free, but what is the value of free? Nothing. If it's free, the prospect will usually think there is a hook, which again goes to pushing as opposed to listening to them. All depends on our attitude and purpose in outbounding.

Have them earn it by giving them an email or filling out a brief survey. If your prospect takes ten seconds to do something, rather than getting something for free, research shows that your results will be improved remarkably. Dropbox got two hundred million users by asking for an account name and password.

More on the do's and don'ts of how to create interest and get off to a great start.

#4 ALL-ABOUT-ME EMAILS

Time and time again, we are asked to review some emails, and time and time again, they look like this.

Hi, (prospect's name). This Is John with XXXXX.

I know I'm calling you out of the blue, and I'll certainly be brief. Can I tell you why I am calling, and you can decide if we have reason to talk further?

The reason for my call is that we've discovered a breakthrough in cloud computing governance and optimization through machine learning. It's been saving our customers 30 to 40 percent on their AWS bill.

Again, I know I'm calling you out of the blue, but can we schedule ten to fifteen minutes to speak in more detail about this on (two business days from now). If you could please respond with one of the following, I'd appreciate it.

Yes—Close now!

Don't care/Not the right person—Ask for referral.

Tell me more.

The reason I ask is because virtually all organizations are using the cloud one way or another. It's seen as more cost effective.

However, cloud costs can accelerate without warning and begin eating into budgets with no clear answer why.

Because of this trend, organizations are now being asked to evaluate their hybrid IT environments and decide what migration, governance, and optimization options are available to them.

From your perspective, looking back at 2019 and forward to the next six months, what are the top three priorities for your organization regarding cloud optimization?

In fact about 83% of workloads will be in cloud by 2020 (Logicmonitor study via Forbes).

This is a real one. Most are not this one-sided, but even this one is an instant delete.

> Hi, Sam,
>
> I love how you're leveraging your experience at eBay and Amazon to drive growth for your brands.
>
> I'm curious if you have ambitions to build a product for the SMB market—helping businesses sell not only through channel partners like Amazon, but also through their own e-commerce sites / physical stores, with pricing and marketing optimized.
>
> We power some of the world's largest e-commerce platforms like YYYY and YYYYY, and I'd love to see how we can help you, too.
>
> What's the best way I can connect with you?

Four "I's," one "we," and three "you's." All you would really have to do to this one is change the perspective and ask questions.

> Hi Sam,
>
> Are you leveraging your experience at eBay and Amazon to drive growth for your brands for the upcoming year?
>
> If you have ambitions to build a product for the SMB market—helping businesses sell not only through channel partners like Amazon, but also through their own e-commerce sites / physical stores—you may want to have a quick conversation with us.
>
> Some of the world's largest e-commerce platforms like YYYY and YYYYY are moving in this direction, and you might want to hear some insightful strategies.

What's the best way to connect with you in the next few days?

Not perfect, but look at the lack of "I's" and more of the "you's." Please proofread your messaging to keep it in your prospects' perspective.

▶ **Quick Story**

When I wrote my first book, *ProActive Sales Management*, I was really proud of the work and was expecting to hear from my editor how good it was.

Well, I heard back. "Skip, we are through the first two chapters and really like the book, but you have used the works "I think" and "I believe" about thirty times already. We know it's what you think and you believe, but you are writing how you speak and not how people read. Please rewrite and get the "I think" and "I believes" out of there.

How right they were.

#5 THE "I" WORD

Reread your email or your phone script. Go back over and get rid of the "I's." General rule: No email should go out using the "I" word more than twice. That includes the words *my* and *our*.

• • •

> Collaboration Words

You need to use "we," "us," "our," and "together," not "you," "I,"
"me," and "your."

Top performing salespeople are up to ten times likelier
to use collaborative words and phrases than low-performing
ones.

Collaborative words increased success rates by 35 percent.

CHAPTER 11

Numbers

Three-quarters of salespeople say their company
provides 25 to 50 percent of their quality leads, which
means you have to get the other 50 percent. Duh!

YOU CAN READ any sales book, and they will tell you
it's a numbers game. They are right. Numbers are only one side
of the equation, though, and you can make numbers look any way
you want. It's a combination of numbers and value that you really
want. First, it's about numbers.

IT'S A NUMBERS GAME

Number of dials, number of connects, number of leads, number
of second conversations, number of demos, and so on. You can
probably measure almost anything you want. What numbers are
important? Well, of course, that depends.

It seems to me over the years that there are a few numbers that can really make or break the outbounding effort.

The Numbers

> ▶ **Skip's Law of Numbers**
>
> Salespeople who do not have enough in their outbound funnel will never make their numbers, regardless of talent. Managers can coach and teach talent. It's up to the salespeople to make sure they don't run dry.

The numbers many companies have are all over the board, depending on what you sell, your Average Selling Price (ASP) or Average Contract Value (ACV), and to whom you are selling.

What we usually see depends on the amount of inbound leads and number of opportunities per rep per territory. With all those disclaimers, here are a few examples.

CASE STUDY 1— TWENTY-FIVE KEY ACCOUNTS STRATEGY— A TEN-DAY SEQUENCE.

Here is a company that sells a lot to mid-market, usually $3,000 to $9,000 MRR (Monthly Reoccurring Revenue), and the reps get about 20 percent of their activity from inbound leads. They identify one persona in their Top 25, and over a two-week calendar window, address that one persona.

Example: The targets are CMOs in the top twenty-five accounts. The Monday/Wednesday/Friday cadence looks like this:

WHAT TO DO:	Day 1	Day 2	Day 3	Day 4	Day 5	WKND
EM - Email	EM1		EM2		EM3	
VM - Voice Mail			VM2			
SM - Social Media						
DM - Direct Mail						
IP - In Person						
TX - Text						
PC - Personal Call			PC2			
VID - 1 Min. Video					VID	
WHAT TO DO:	WKND	Day 6	Day 7	Day 8	Day 9	Day 10
EM - Email				EM3		EM4
VM - Voice Mail		VM3				VM4
SM - Social Media						
DM - Direct Mail						
IP - In Person						
TX - Text						
PC - Personal Call		PC3				PC4
VID - 1 Min. Video						

On Monday, the CMO will get an email. On Wednesday, a phone call and an email. On Friday, an email and a video. (The video is less than one minute, is personalized, and has some homework information in it. It is also sent through LinkedIn SanNavigator, so it gets past spam filters.)

This two-week cadence stops at the end of the two weeks, rests for two to four weeks, then starts up again. The thinking is that every month is a new month, and priorities usually get adjusted either on a monthly or quarterly basis, so play into the customer's priorities.

The other cadence is the Tuesday/Thursday cadence. Let's assume they also want to try to reach the CIO. The alternate day cadence for their top-twenty-five accounts would look like this:

WHAT TO DO:	Day 1	Day 2	Day 3	Day 4	Day 5	WKND
EM - Email		EM1		EM2	EM3	
VM - Voice Mail				VM2		
SM - Social Media						
DM - Direct Mail						
IP - In Person						
TX - Text						
PC - Personal Call				PC2		
VID - 1 Min. Video					VID	

WHAT TO DO:	WKND	Day 6	Day 7	Day 8	Day 9	Day 10
EM - Email					EM3	EM4
VM - Voice Mail			VM3		VM4	
SM - Social Media						
DM - Direct Mail						
IP - In Person						

WHAT TO DO (continued):	WKND	Day 6	Day 7	Day 8	Day 9	Day 10
TX - Text						
PC - Personal Call			PC3		PC4	
VID - 1 Min. Video						

Same number of touches, but on alternate dates, except for Fridays. Again, these numbers and touches can be changed to fit the territory. This runs for two weeks, gets a two- to four-week rest, then resumes.

Note: During the rest, another targeted persona is started. There is never a time when there are not twenty-five active cadences going. Do the math:

▸ Twelve touches over two weeks to twenty-five ATL prospects is 12 x 2 x 25 = 600 touches every two weeks, or 300/week or 1,200/month

▸ That's fifty ATL/BTL people contacted every two weeks (2 cadences x 25 contacts)

▸ With an average response rate of 10 to 20 percent. That's five to ten new leads every two weeks or ten to twenty per month.

▸ Thirty-plus percent will turn into a decision, so five or six per month

▸ The average sale is $5,000/month, so $5,000 x (five or six deals) is $25,000 to $30,000/month new business.

▸ There is a 10 to 20 percent residual slippage, so every month has old leads (one or two contacts and then a week or two dark). These are in-process leads that are still active and new leads generated.

▸ Every month, the salesperson can get $25,000 to $30,000 of new business and $25,000 to $30,000 of old leads' new business. This cadence sequence will generate $50,000 to $60,000/month of new business, not counting other outbounding efforts and inbound leads.

▸ With a new business quota of $500,000/year, these numbers add up to making quota without counting any inbound leads.

Additionally, the time required for this activity is usually less than two hours per day. There may be a heavy day when a salesperson actually gets three to five callbacks in one day, so sometimes it goes over the two-hour/day mark, but rarely.

Remember, the goal is not a long conversation, the goal is to set up a next meeting, so the two-hour/day rule is usually a safe bet. There is no doubt that reps who work these numbers will get the most connects. Connects lead to next steps, which is usually a meeting, a presentation, a demo, or whatever. Salespeople who get the most next-step meetings usually are at the top of the leaderboard. Period.

Know your numbers.

CASE STUDY #2

This example has a salesperson selling a $80,000 to $100,000 ARR (Annual Reoccurring Revenue) product. They focus on ten accounts per two-week cadence. In this case study, the message on the email or the voice mail always references the last touch, so there is rapport building up.

The cadence looks like this:

WHAT TO DO:	Day 1	Day 2	Day 3	Day 4	Day 5	WKND
EM - Email	EM1		EM2		EM3	
VM - Voice Mail	VM1					
SM - Social Media						
DM - Direct Mail						
IP - In Person						
TX - Text						
PC - Personal Call	PC1					
VID - 1 Min. Video					VID	
WHAT TO DO:	WKND	Day 6	Day 7	Day 8	Day 9	Day 10
EM - Email				EM4		EM5
VM - Voice Mail		VM2				VM3
SM - Social Media						
DM - Direct Mail						
IP - In Person						
TX - Text						
PC - Personal Call		PC2				PC3
VID - 1 Min. Video						

• • •

The messages go something like this after the first one.

PC1 after EM1

Hi, John.

I tried to get ahold of you today via email. Hope you get a chance to read it. It should be of interest to you. I will try you again this Wednesday.

Thanks.

EM2

Hi, John,

Trying you again. Please see below the reason I would like to get ten minutes on your calendar. If you can let me know what time works for you, that would be great.
I'll try you again on Friday if I don't hear from you.

Talk soon.

And so on. They always reference the past and future attempts, so really, there is a rapport that is starting to happen; curiosity by the prospect, and in a strange way, it's the start of a give/get relationship.

The numbers also add up for this example.

▸ Eleven touches over two weeks to ten ATL prospects is 11 x 2 x 10 = 220 touches every two weeks, or 110/week or 440/month.
▸ That's twenty ATL/BTL people contacted every two weeks.

▶ With an average response rate of 10 to 20 percent, that's two to three new leads every two weeks, or four to six per month.

▶ Thirty-plus percent will turn into a decision, so one to two per month.

▶ The average sale is $80,000, so $80,000 x (1 or 2 deals) is $80,000 to $160,000 new business.

▶ That's 1.5 deals per month x $80,000 is $1.2 million in the pipeline on an annual quota of $800,000 per year.

Again, not counting inbound leads. Numbers don't lie. You need numbers at the top of your funnel to make it, no matter how good you think you are.

General rules about using numbers and making assumptions.

▶ It takes longer to sell high dollar than low dollar deals.

▶ It takes longer to sell to BTL than to ATL.

▶ Selling to .gov, .org, and .edu usually takes longer.

▶ Bottom-up selling, BTL to ATL, usually takes longer than top-down ATL to BTL does. You do have to get the messaging right. Kid table and adult table, right?

NUMBERS AND VALUE

Certain numbers have more value than others. What is of value early in the sales process? Where should you spend quality time?

Understanding outcomes—big one, right here. Both the BTL and ATL buyers have outcomes they want for any investment they will be making. These outcomes usually have numbers that imply value. Remember, ATL rarely cares about BTL numbers, and vice versa. BTL is going to use it, so what's important?

Go back to the 5Ps model (see my book *ProActive Selling* for more definition here).

▶ Product Features
▶ Product Quality
▶ Professional Support
▶ Price
▶ Perceived Image (Brand)

Come up with a list of important items in each of these categories for your BTL buyer.

▶ I'm tired of working eighty-hour weeks.
▶ It has to be 50 percent more reliable than we have now.
▶ I can never get any help when I need it. It usually takes two to three days.
▶ Ease of use—20 percent less time
▶ Reliability—5,000 hours between services
▶ Service—Response time within four hours

ATLs have trains they need to get out of the station. Getting the size of their problem and the size of their outcome are critical. Stay focused on ValueStar (see *ProActive Selling* on the five value points for an ATL).

▶ ROI (on their train/gap, not on your stuff)
▶ Time
▶ Risk
▶ Leverage (ability to hit multiple trains)
▶ Brand (internal and external)

Some examples of needed value numbers to them, not your value, would be:

▶ We have a 20 percent gap in our revenue expectations.
▶ We need to shave three months off the process.
▶ I need to have 20 percent more production capacity by the end of the year.
▶ We have 20 to 30 percent too much risk in these results.
▶ I have 75 percent confidence in these plans.
▶ I need an answer that can affect all three plants. I'm tired of three different solutions. It's costing us 20 percent production time.

▶ The Numbers #1 Rule

If you don't know the desired size of the outcome, how do you determine the size of the solution you are offering?

The sooner the ATL is onboard and can identify that what you are selling can affect their trains and gaps, the better, but you need to quantify it. ATLs always work with numbers.

Numbers don't lie. Numbers are a gateway to urgency. There is a reason the train is in the station, and if it gets out of the station, it will be making money for the company. ATL and BTL know their numbers, and you need to, too. If you can make a dent in a $30 million problem, and your cost is $5,000/month, you don't need a calculator to determine ROI, and a $30 million problem usually gets attention.

YOUR DAILY NUMBERS

Noting daily activity and summing up to daily/weekly goals is a great way to keep your head down and fill your pipeline. What to measure is up to you, but take some time and develop the ProActive Outbound Scorecard.

In this Scorecard, the salesperson puts value on:

▸ Calls attempted
▸ Calls completed and have at least a two-minute duration
▸ ATL and BTL numbers. What is the size of the problem?
▸ Agreed to next steps, within a five-day window.

It's a simple scorecard, but reps need this at their desk and need to review it with their manager every day. It's like a daily log. Now each salesperson should also have a daily goal, based on points. There are a bunch of options on how to hit your daily and weekly goals, and it should allow you the flexibility and creativity to reach those goals.

ProActive Outbound Scorecard–Bill Smith

Activity	Value	QTY	Day 1	QTY	Day 2	QTY	Day 3	QTY	Day 4	QTY	Day 5	SUM
Calls Attempted	0.1	20	2	30	3							
Calls Completed (2 Minutes+)	0.5	20	0		0							
Cadence Activity	0.1	20	2	22	2.2							
ATL Numbers	5	5	25	2	10							
BTL Numbers	2	5	10	7	14							
ATL Next Step (5 Days)	5	1	5	2	10							
BTL Next Step (5 Days)	3		0	2	6							
Daily Total			44		45.2		0		0		0	89.2
Daily Goal			50		50		50		50		50	250
% of Goal			88%		90%		0%		0%		0%	36%

Bill, the salesperson, has completed two days so far this week. Even by just looking at the totals for two days, you can make some assumptions.

▶ He's below his goals.
▶ He's really good at getting ATL and BTL numbers.
▶ He's doing well on his cadences and call attempts.
▶ More calls completed and ATL numbers will help get him over his weekly goals.

By managing this scoresheet, Bill can self-determine what he needs to do to get his scores up. Over time, score values can change based on activity and goals. It's all about activity and value.

ProActive Outbound Scorecard

Using this daily scorecard will make sure that you stay focused on the key accounts. You could use this for your top twenty-five accounts, making sure you go broad and deep in each account by persona.

TIME MANAGEMENT

One more time on Important vs Urgent. Great salespeople use PowerHour and the ProActive Sales Matrix to their advantage. (See ProActive Selling for more info on these tools.) It's focusing on the important stuff that you commit to and not being distracted by "urgent" stuff that you might feel good about doing, but does not make a dent on your important stuff.

Without focusing on what's important and using these tools, outbounding is usually sent to the back burner, a "I have to get to it" mentality, and, guess what—numbers are never achieved.

CHAPTER 12

Homework and Preparation

There's a clear relationship between the number of questions reps ask and their chances of success. You need to be intermittently asking questions to the buyer.

THE NEED FOR HOMEWORK

During my research phase for this book, I interviewed quite a few successful reps, managers, and vice presidents to get a good grasp on what successful salespeople do when they outbound.

There are several trends, but the glaring one, the one most stressed by almost all the people I talked to, was homework—the need to do real research and good-quality homework.

Most successful organizations did not really rely on purchased lists. It seems that in the fast-changing world we live in, there is usually a lot of movement in the ATL and BTL world, so looking up on the website to get the most current ATL executives, and researching tools like LinkedIn to get the most current BTL folks, is a must do. Other takeaways:

▸ Bad contact information for people who have left the company can create some negative energy and wasted time. Make sure as best as you can to target only current employees.

▸ When researching, look for rapport items like companies they know that you know, people you know that they know, schools, locations, anything that can spark some rapport with the prospect.

▸ Homework on recent blogs, articles, or posts the prospect has made is invaluable.

Homework for Small and Midsize Prospects

The words *fast* and *furious* describe this effort. When targeting small and midsize companies, fifteen minutes per prospect is a lot of time.

▸ Google their name and company
▸ Company website
▸ LinkedIn
▸ Quora
▸ PR and news releases
▸ Annual reports—especially the chairman's message and the area of risks
▸ Company Twitter and Facebook pages

That's about it. If you are in transactional sales, LinkedIn, company website, that's about it. Don't overthink it. If it could be a real important account for you, OK, thirty minutes.

Homework for Enterprise Prospects

Enterprise homework is similar to small and midsize companies, but in more detail.

▶ Read the annual reports—go back two to three years and notice trends, who has been around that long, and who is new.
▶ Glassdoor.com (a website where current and former employees anonymously review companies) will address culture.
▶ Look at your own CRM (Customer Relationship Management) and Marketing Automation System for retouch possibilities.

The goal, once again, is to find out what trains are in the station, and what gaps do they have that are still in the station. This goes for company trains and personal ATL trains. Also remember, goals should align upward. If an ATL has a train in the station, it usually will align to one of their boss's trains. Use these ideas to spark curiosity and build rapport in your outbounding efforts.

PART 3

On Your Mark, Get Set . . .

Most salespeople make 70 percent more calls in the last month of the quarter than the first two. The success rate of those "end of the quarter" calls are lower than any other month.

This section focuses on being prepared. Tactical listening skills, developing a focus for your messaging, how to organize a call, and overcoming initial objections.

CHAPTER 13

Tactical Listening Skills

Listening is like playing an instrument. The more you intentionally practice, the better you get.

LISTENING IS HARD. No, really hard. Hearing is easy. Here is the difference between the two.

Hearing is the "process, function, or power of perceiving sound; specifically: the special sense by which noises and tones are received as stimuli."

Listening is "to pay attention to sound; to hear something with thoughtful attention; and to give consideration."

What a difference. Hearing is something that just happens, but listening requires some work. Additionally, there two different types of listening, active and passive.

ACTIVE LISTENING

Active listening can be defined as "a way of listening and responding to another person that improves mutual understanding." In other words, active listening is about being curious.

Passive listening is something you do all the time, you are hearing and trying to understand the speaker and words, but they are not making a connection in your brain.

Active listening is the way you want to listen if you're really seeking to understand another person or you're looking for a solution. It's a good skill for salespeople and especially a needed skill set for salespeople who outbound. Why? Because when someone is having a communication with another person, you can always tell if someone is not actively listening to you.

You can tell if someone's really listening or not, because the other person, who always has an agenda, will dominate the conversation to make sure that he or she get to address that agenda. Pauses will happen at inopportune times, and there will be a lot of "yeahs" and "uh-huhs."

Additionally, if someone is actively listening, they should be able to hold on for a minute or two before they interrupt. If the person you are having a conversation with continues to interrupt you, it's a strong sign that they are not hearing what you are saying.

A way for you to make sure someone is really listening to you is to ask them questions back. When someone is listening, you should be able to give them a quiz about what you just said. Ask, "What do you think about what we have just been discussing?" or, "How would what we've just been discussing help you?"

If they are not actively listening, they will give you a weird answer like, "That's great," or, "Right." To get their attention, try to get agreement on a topic to discuss so you know you can continue the conversation, stay in control, and know you will be talking with someone who is more engaged.

FILTERS

Be aware that you actually have listening filters that you may want to keep in check, or the person you will be talking to on the phone will know you are not listening. Filters include:

▶ Pretend Listening—This is where you are pretending to listen, but you really are just waiting for an opportunity to jump in and speak.

▶ Key Word Listening—This is where you are listening for a key word to jump in. "We really are interested in data for the mobile space . . ." "Mobile? Well, let me tell you what we have in mobile."

▶ Self-Centered Listening—This is where you really are only listening to things about you or what you can affect. Also called egoistical listening.

These filters stop you from actively listening, and you should try really hard to overcome them. *Listen to what the other person is saying.* You'll find it hard because those filters are powerful.

Finally, make sure when you are listening, you are not passing Judgment. Some Judgment filters include:

▶ Instructing: "If I were you . . . ," "Why didn't you . . . ?" (challenging)

▶ Do Better: "Really? Well, let me tell you what I did . . ." (hijacking)

▸ Overeducating: "So, here are three ways you need to . . ."
  (rambling)
▸ Personal Story-topping: "That's a good one. I was there,
  too, but I can improve on that . . ." (discounting)
▸ Clarifying: "What I would have done is . . ."
  (disregarding)
▸ Correcting: "That's not what happened . . ."
  (confrontational)

Bottom line: To quote Tony Robbins, "Effective listening requires an understanding that it is your responsibility that the other person feels understood."

INTERRUPTIONS

Simply put, when you are interrupting someone, you are telling them, "I'm more important than you are." How would you feel if you were talking to someone and that person said or implied that what you had to say was not interesting? Yet you continue to interrupt people, because "If I can take what's in my head, and put it in your head, you'll see my point of view." Nah, doesn't work like that.

When you interrupt, you are loudly saying, "I don't care what you think and I don't have time for your opinion." Not really a place you want to be. Try not to interrupt. (Of course, for the person who won't shut up and has no direction for conversation, just get off the phone. They won't be buying from you anyway.)

WHAT PROSPECTS WANT TO HEAR OR READ

For the ATL buyer, you need to focus on what is of importance to them.

ATL Focus

▶ Make or save money—It's all about revenue and earnings. Most ATLs talk to you about where they need to make money and why it's not doing well (away), rather than a blanket statement of, "We can make you more money" (toward).

▶ Save time—It's not really about "saving time," it's about "stop wasting time" (away). Most ATL trains that are in the train station are talking too long. The market is moving fast and they are missing it. Ask questions about the lack of time, rather than getting more time.

▶ Reduce risk—It is all about risk, but getting to this when outbounding can be tricky. Most ATL buyers want to talk about their risks, but only if they have some rapport with you. When you outbound, don't lead with risk. Ask about trains and time travel, then go to risk. "Ms. Jones, regarding that project that is three months behind schedule, what risk do you see for the company if you don't make up that time?" They will talk, and talk, and talk.

BTL Focus

The BTL buyer is a feature/function person. They want it to work better, stop breaking, avoid having to answer questions that they are supposed to know but don't have the tools to get them.

▶ Faster/easier/better—This usually works to get a BTL's attention. Remember, you have to be solving a problem, so you might get their attention with (toward) statements, but you will get them talking with (away) questions.

▶ Stop wasting time, stop working so hard, stop working with stuff that doesn't really work—These are the people on the front lines, they will be responsible for whatever you are selling to work. It's going to be more emotional than for the ATL buyer. Don't be afraid to ask these emotional questions, especially, "What's in it for you for this change to happen?"

▶ The BTL Buying Story

For years, I had the honor of attending a certain company's Sales Kick Off (SKO), and each year, they would have a guest speaker who typically was a senior BTL buyer. Each year, a different speaker from a different company would get up there and give a story on how well they used the product they bought, and no matter who the speaker or what company they were from, the speaker would cry. No, they would cry.

"I bought your software a few years ago, and it was like night and day from what I was doing before. I guess I was so happy with it, I would brag about this software to anyone who would listen.

I live in Portland, and we have a big manufacturing plant in Nashville. The plant was having a major failure rate on some its parts, and this was causing millions of dollars in lost sales and an increase in manufacturing reruns and overhead costs. They asked me if I could pinpoint the problems.

So, me, the plant manager, and a general manager fly on the private jet. I've never been on a private jet before. So, on the way to Nashville, I got some plant data, and using your software, I found the problems before we even landed. We went to the plant, agreed on what the problems were and how to fix them, and I was able to get on a plane that night and did not have to spend the weekend in Nashville solving problems.

Because I got home Friday night, I was able to see my son's first Little League game, and it's something. I told him . . . since he was young . . . that I would never miss . . . *BAH-HHHHH.*" He starts crying, the audience starts crying. Yep, every year the same thing happens.

BTL buyers are emotionally attached to the thing you are selling. If true, then they are emotionally attached to the thing that is holding them back.

PROBLEMS PER PERSONA

Finally, make sure you look at the title of the person you are going to contact and make some assumptions, especially at the ATL level.

(CEO): big picture, quickly. Tasked with getting the highest possible revenues while not compromising on performance. They want to know the essentials—so get to the point.

(CFO): prove the bottom-line benefit. You need to be focused around increase revenues as well as reduce expense. Prove the return on investment and how it affects trains in the organization. ROI for the product or service you are selling is easily dismissed. You need to show how it helps current initiatives.

(CIO): benefit versus risk. Technology is changing rapidly and advances and disruption are everywhere. Many are struggling to get rid of their legacy systems. They need to maintain and keep legacy systems running, while providing the latest technology to employees. Risk and time.

(CMO): revenue, market share, brand, and leads. The CMO now spends more on technology than the CIO. They are the engine that drives the sales revenue train. They never have enough revenue, always are hurting to gain market share faster than their competitors, and their Net Promoter Score will tell them how their product is doing and what their brand is doing for them.

Oh, and don't forget the millions they are spending on leads (the sales department is still complaining).

There are many more ATL titles. You should do your homework before you outbound to them so your messaging is focused on what they want to hear.

WHAT IS THE SIZE OF THE PROBLEM?

If you want to sum it up, customers, both ATL and BTL, want to talk about their problems, what's holding them back in their job, from obtaining their goals, and, "what keeps them awake at night," so to speak.

You want to let them talk about their needs, problems and concerns in the hopes that you might help them solve their problem, and maybe buy something from you along the way.

You also want to know if this effort has energy, if both parties start down an investigation buy/sales path, so that at the finish line, the customer does just go dark and say: "Now's not the right time. Maybe next year when we can get a budget."

How do you do that? You have a mission, and that mission is a very simple one.

What's the size of the problem?

Can't get easier than that. If they have a problem that is costing them $50/month, and you come in with a solution that can help them at $1,000/month, this deal doesn't make sense, and you can tell that early on, so you don't waste a lot of time and effort.

However, if the customer has a problem that is costing them $10,000/month, and what you offer can get rid of this problem at $500/month, what are we talking about here?

What really slays me here is a solution you have at $500/month, which is $6,000/year, that will help the prospect save $120,000/year, you will discount at the end of the month just to get the deal, because you don't have the numbers of the size of the problem.

"OK, Mary, our solution is $6,000/year. I know that is a competitive price, but if you decide this month, we will do the deal at $5,000."

The sales team, yes, salesperson and manager, have just given away $1,000 of margin, not revenue, but margin. Man, that will make CFOs roll over in their grave. Why do sales teams do this? Again, they don't know the size of the problem.

▶ "They have a major problem."

▸ "This is a key initiative."

▸ "Our solution is worth a ton. That's what they said."

▸ "Really, this is their main problem."

OK, quantify these. You can't. It's all subjective. (How much is a ton worth?) Because you don't know the size of the problem, you are going to go down a buy/sales path, and maybe waste a lot of time, and discount at the end, because you don't know the answer to this simple question. Oh, and by the way, typically, the BTL is involved with features and benefits and has received a budget from the ATL. They are not involved with the size of the problem discussions.

If you want an outbounding mission statement, it's: What's the size of the problem?

Quick note: Remember Solution Boxes, especially Solution Box B. You will not be the entire answer for Solution Box B, you just have to be a part of it, make a dent in it, for you to be considered a viable solution. How much of a dent? That has to come from the ATL. Ask—if he or she can't tell you, go back to square one.

What's the size of the problem? Memorize this. It will open ATL doors.

EXAMPLE 1

Keith has a deal he just researched, and he feels this can be a really good one. He started a cadence to the ATL, and after two emails and one call, he received a reply that said, "Let's talk."

The call went well. Keith said that Sarah, the ATL, was interested in starting a process. They are currently using a competitor and are not happy with it.

"Every week I hear of problems. It's time we looked at doing something different." Keith said. "That's why I scheduled her for a demonstration on Thursday."

Dan, the sales manager, listens intently, and when Keith is done, asks: "It looks like we have good ATL involvement right from the start. What's the size of Sarah's problem?"

"I knew you were going to ask that, Dan. She said it costs her money every week, and she no longer can afford to lose this kind of money."

"So how much is she losing every week?" Dan asked.

"Well, I don't have an exact figure, but you can tell from how she talked about it, it's really important, and she agreed to a demo this Thursday," Keith proclaimed.

"Keith, you know the rules. First, if it's an ATL, she knows the size of the problem. She probably has a slide in her executive quarterly update presentation on it. Ask for it. Second, if we don't know the size of the problem, how can we offer a solution, and third, if Sarah has not identified a quantifiable problem, she won't spend any money on it."

"Dan, you're right. I got so excited, I forgot to get those numbers. I'll call Sarah, confirm our time and agenda on Thursday, and ask her for a quantified problem. I'll see if I can get that slide too."

"Perfect, and I'll be surprised if she doesn't have one."

EXAMPLE 2

"So, Kelley, I think that about covers it. You said you have a problem and you need it fixed by the end of the quarter, and I said that we can help with that, so I think we have had a good meeting. Any questions?"

"Yes, Elizabeth, what does your solution roughly cost?"

"Good question, and the answer of course depends on the size of the problem. We can offer a good/better/best solution, but don't want to oversize or undersize a solution that would create problems later. If I can ask you a question, what is the size of the problem?"

"That's fair. Well, given we need $10 million from this product line this coming fiscal year, and if we don't solve this problem, I see us finishing the year with only half that, so really, I have a $5 million revenue gap. But, Elizabeth, you won't get me the whole $5 million."

"I realize that," said Elizabeth, "but how much of the $5 million do you think this will help you?"

"Well, that depends of course, but if you can do what we just discussed, I can see you're worth at least half of the $5 million."

"Perfect, so our options are $1,000/month, $5,000/month, and a yearly subscription price of $75,000. We can figure out which makes sense for you right now or at our next meeting if that's OK with you."

Remember to ask questions, and to ask for the size of the problem. It's a good qualifying question, and a way to determine if your outbounding efforts for this deal should be continued.

3-1-2

You now have your mission statement, What's the size of the problem, and now it's time for you to get ready for your outbound attempt. How do you prepare for this?

You are going to start an outbound cadence this Monday. An email, a phone call, or a social media attempt, it doesn't matter, it's a sales call. As you know, there are three parts to a sales call. Here are the three elements.

▶ 1—The Intro—This is how you kick off the sales call. That first minute or two to set the stage, or the first few sentences of the email.
▶ 2—The Middle—This is the content of the sales call. What you are planning to talk about. Typically, the agenda for the meeting.
▶ 3—The End—This is how you wrap it up and control the next step in the process.

If all great sales calls start with the end in mind, the correct order to plan for the call is: 3-1-2.

You start with the last element first. Before you even think about the Intro or the Middle, you must think:

"If this call goes well, if I get a response to the email, what is the next step I want to have happen? What is the best outcome for all parties, and what is our next step? What does each of us need to do when this meeting is over?"

Yes, this sounds a little backward, but if you don't have a goal or a direction you want this call to go and where you want it to end up, you will end up directionless, which of course is not good, since then someone other than you can take control of this sale, which would be bad.

▶ **Buyers Want to Be Led**

Someone will have to take control of this sale, and most buyers don't really know how to buy. They have a problem, and if you let them talk about their problem and offer a way to help them solve it, they will let you lead. If they knew how to solve it, they wouldn't be talking to you, now, would they?

Every sale and every sales call needs a leader. Leaders know up front what they want their outcome to be. That's not to say during the call, other options may come up that would certainly be better than the one you planned for. That's good, and you now need a structure to plan for the end of the call, as well as to modify the end if, during the meeting, something comes up.

If you want to start with the end in mind, you have to plan for it, really think about it. There is so much going on, especially when you are going to be doing a presentation, a demonstration, or trying to qualify. You are so busy trying to accomplish the task at hand, you forget that you are on a journey. Build the sales cadences backward, and each attempt in the cadence, you should be asking yourself, what is the outcome I want? Ask yourself, really ask yourself:

"If this attempt goes well, and I get a response, what is the next step for everyone—me, the ATL, and the BTL. What are the next steps?"

Once you have those outcomes, then you can build the outline of what you want to have happen at each step in the sales cadence.

For a sales call where you have some rapport, finish the 3-1-2 model. Plan for the beginning and say, "If all goes well, a good next step could be a. . . ." Use the direction in step three in the introduction.

Execute a call 1-2-3. Plan for a call 3-1-2.

CHAPTER 14

Trains and Gaps

More than half of inbound prospects want to see a demo on the first call. Less than 10 percent of outbound prospects want to see one on the first call. Uh-oh.

YOUR MISSION

Putting this all together, what's the mission you are on? You have to have a mission. OK, try this one out. When outbounding, we've established your mission is to find out:

What is the size of the problem?

This one sentence can tell you a lot.

▸ Is there energy for this deal?
▸ How serious is the customer?

▶ Is this a prospect worth spending time on?

▶ Is the customer ready to change?

▶ Is the ATL involved?

We have made numerous references to trains and gaps throughout this book so far. This is why: By hunting for trains and identifying gaps, you can outbound to an ATL to get to the answers to your mission statement.

In *Selling Above and Below the Line*, the analogy of trains was brought up. To review, think of ATL buyers as train station masters. They have initiatives (trains) that they have committed to their company they will do. Typical business initiatives would be:

▶ Increase revenue by 20 percent.

▶ Hire fifteen more people by June.

▶ Develop and start Asia/Pacific Channel and have $10 million in revenue by the end of the year.

▶ Generate 40 percent more leads through social media channels.

Let's call these initiatives "trains." The ATL buyer has these trains, and some are looking great and are out making money. Next quarter, new trains will be coming into the station. There are some initiatives, though, that need help. They are not fully baked yet. Let's call these trains in the train station.

You, Bob, make a call to Mary, an ATL, and ask her what her issues, challenges, concerns are, and she will tell you about one of her trains.

"I need to lower my customer acquisition cost (CAC) by 20 percent for Q2, and I'm stuck on how to do that without cutting heads."

Well, it just so happens, you have something that might help her in this area.

"Mary, that's an interesting dilemma. Let me ask you, how much of the 20 percent do you still need?"

"Great question," says Mary, "Right now, I can see my way to about 5 percent without having to lay some people off" (size of the problem).

Mary and Bob then have a discussion and realize there might be a reason to investigate what Bob's company has to offer. This is going to be the start of a good sales situation.

When outbounding, you need to hunt for trains and find out why that train is in the train station. It's where your prospect's energy is being spent, and therefore a good outbounding candidate.

MULTIPLE TRAINS

To act out the role play from above, if you can influence one train, Mary will say, "I have assigned Kurt to be the leader of this project, so why don't you work with Kurt and see what you can do?"

All very logical, but as soon as you call Kurt up and have some discussions, good luck getting back to Mary (going over Kurt's head, bad move).

What you should have done was hunt for multiple trains. Why? Because Mary builds value over multiple trains.

Let's assume Mary has four trains in her train station. She tells you about the train on track one. Instead of jumping on that train, why don't you ask: "Thanks, Mary, for that one train. Are there any others?"

If you do that and determine that you can make a dent in two or three trains that Mary has in her station, watch how fast this outbound lead becomes a sale.

Observation: It never ceases to amaze me how the trains concept is understood so well, but when I get involved in account reviews, it's always the same.

"OK, Skip, I got this deal I'm working on that. I could use some help," Kevin, a pretty good commercial sales rep, said to me the other day.

"OK, tell me about it."

"This is a pretty big deal. My ATL contact is Ron, and my BTL contact is Deb. It's about a $200,000 deal for us. They want our product ABC and want to use it in at least five locations. The demo went great, and we are in the final proposal stage, and. . . ."

"STOP," I cut in. "First, what is the size of the problem?"

"I knew you were going to ask me that. The answer is Ron needs $25 million in new revenue, and he believes he's going to be about 25 percent short."

"Great. Nice job. What other trains have you found?"

"No, Skip, this is the reason why they are looking at us," Kevin firmly stated.

"You mean to tell me that your ATL, Ron, only has one train in his station. There are no other initiatives he's working on? Nothing else?"

"Well, he may be working on other stuff, but all I know is this is the one that I'm concerned about, since it can mean a big sale for me."

"Hold on, Kevin," I said. "What if Ron has three or four other initiatives that he is working on, trains in his train station, and what if we could make a dent in some of those? What if Ron could get added benefit from making a decision in our favor?"

"Well, he would probably have to spend a little more money, but not a ton more. Also, for one decision, he could make dents in a few trains, which Ron would probably like, since it would get more trains out of his train station." Kevin asserted.

"Exactly. Now, how much does your BTL, Deb, know about other things that Ron is working on?"

"Probably not much, since they actually sit in different buildings. She's never brought up any other trains, so I never asked for any."

"Kevin, you now have a single-train solution for a pretty big-sized deal. That's a risky position to be in, and, quite frankly, if your customers can get a bigger benefit out of their investment with you, but you didn't bring that up, are you really doing your job?"

"Oh, man, good point. I need to get ahold of Ron right now and see what other trains are in his station, because if we can help with even one more, it will give us a great leg up on the competition."

"Yep, you're getting it."

Hunting for multiple trains will mean bigger opportunities, and you create a win/win for both you and your prospect.

PART 4

Go

You can plan all you want—there comes a time to execute. Use all the tools we have discussed and jump in the pool. The water's fine.

CHAPTER 15

Outbounding

More than 60 percent of salespeople don't outbound enough to meet the number of leads they need. They end up failing to make quota. Geez. That means you just have to show up most of the time, and you are worried about what to say!

IF YOU ARE going to dive in and start outbounding, let's go to your cadences.

Opening up with a phone call or an email is entirely up to you. Some salespeople want to let the prospect know they are coming, some feel better just jumping on a call.

The next section has some specific tools for outbounding on the phone, so let's wait for that. Right now, let's get ready for the process, email and social communications, and objection handling.

• • •

> ▶ WARNING. WARNING
>
> OK, you are ready to go. Remember, you are not selling anyone anything yet. You are just looking for some time to find out what their trains are and why they are in the station. The goal is a next step, not a contract and commission. This is a first date, not a marriage proposal.

TOOLS AVAILABLE FOR THE FIRST CONTACT

Email and social contact goals may be the same thing. In social contact, your message must be really short, and for an email, you need to be less than 120 words and no more than one swipe on a mobile device. Some basic hints:

▶ The goal of an email or social touch is to get it opened.

▶ The goal of the first sentence is to get the second one read.

▶ Prospect about change and outcomes. No one wants to talk about you and what you are offering, yet.

▶ Time travel with ATLs.

▶ Be more away than toward.

▶ Confidence comes through your messaging. You are hunting for their initiatives and finding out why they are still in the train station. They want to talk to you about themselves, because they need to get their initiatives out of the train station.

THE INTRODUCTION EMAIL

The typical introduction email should be something like this:

▸ Subject line—The simple subject line, the one-word subject line, or the number subject line are all good. Personalization can really help. Write your subject line after you write your email; you'll get more ideas.

▸ Introduction—"Hello, John (be careful when using first names unless you are sure they go by that name. My real name is William, but I go by Skip. Any email I get that says "Hello, Bill" is an instant delete for me).

▸ Using first name or first and last name is a personal preference. Both are OK.

▸ Curiosity—Remember this is a top way to get someone's attention. Get me curious about me, my job, my company, my LinkedIn blogs, the industry I'm in, time, or where I live.

▸ Names/Numbers—Your prospect will be drawn to a name, if they recognize it, or numbers in digit form.

▸ Call to action—What do you want them to do?

PUT IT ALL TOGETHER

Subject Line: 3 Actions That Can't Wait

John,

As the quarter ends, CMOs are asking, "How can I do more in the next two quarters without an increase in spend?"
    Here are three things you can do:

1. Layoff 30 percent of your workforce
2. Work more weekends
3. Use marketing organization tools that eliminate redundant work

As you figured out, we have tools for #3. Who in your organization should I quickly talk with to do some initial investigation?

Seventy-two words. Short and to the point. You should change this up to fit your personality. Read some articles on the web and research some of the thousands of articles and blogs on what to do and what not to do. The goal?

▸ 35 percent open rates for emails are a standard you should shoot for.
▸ Set up further touches in your cadence.

Do not expect a return email or callback on the first outreach. Oh, it can happen, but in reality, work your cadence.

TRUMPETING, TRUMPETING UP, TRUMPETING ASK

If you really want to focus your initial outbounding on ATLs, use trumpeting. When you are starting to prospect, either outbound or inbound, and before you contact any BTL user, you send an email or social media message to three to four top ATLs in the company.

Inbound example:

Dear Mary, Jane, Freda, Bill,

We just received an inquiry from your company. We plan to follow up on this, and if there is a financial reason or a real issue that can be impacted, I'll send you more information. Thanks in advance.

Regards,
Skip Miller
Account Manager
XYZ Company

Outbound example:

Dear Mary, Jane, Freda, Bill,

After looking at your website and some financial information, and based on the industry you are in, there may be a financial reason or a real issue that can be impacted with a quick fifteen-minute discussion.

I'll send you some more information before I call so you can make an early decision. Thanks in advance.

Regards,
Skip Miller
Account Manager
XYZ Company

You would not believe the hallway and back-channel conversations that go on after a trumpet is sent out. Mary gets this and says to herself, what do Jane, Freda and Bill know that I don't know? They all ask themselves this. Trumpeting creates curiosity, and it's is a legitimate email.

Most ATL executives want to be kept informed. On the inbound trumpet, that's all you are doing here. You are letting them know that if this is important, and it needs their attention, you'll let them know. It's a status update, and what ATL exec doesn't want to have the status of something updated with them? It is also a great way to create noise, which is what a trumpet does.

You want to send this to three or four, not two, not five, all addressed to the same group. No addressing to one and cc the others. Use this: "To: Mary, Jane, Freda, Bill."

Try some different spins.

▸ Have the letter come from your boss or even your president.
▸ Use some customers' names to show you are in good company.
▸ Tie it to an event, yours or theirs.
▸ Use the buyer's calendar to tie it to business events on a quarterly basis.

On the outbound trumpet, you are letting them know you have done some homework and there may be a reason to talk. That's it, that's all you are doing. You are creating noise, and it's a good way to start your cadences. The rest of your touches should be individual touches. You've already created the noise, the attention.

Trumpeting is another example of prospecting tools that work, and most sales organizations don't try, because they outbound to the BTL and wouldn't dare go around the person who has made the initial contact or go over the head of a past contact. They want to talk to someone who can talk about products and services, not about outcomes. Well, time to change that up.

Trumpeting Up

Another example of Trumpeting is called Trumpeting Up.

> Dear Mary, Jane, Freda, Bill,
>
> We are in the process of contacting Larry Hughes, your manager of IT marketing, for your marketing lead-generation issues. We plan on staying with this, and if there is a financial reason or a real issue that can be impacted, I'll send you more information.
>
> Please let us know if there are other people involved in this process we should reach out to.
>
> > Thanks in advance,
> > Skip Miller
> > Account Manager
> > XYZ Company

The goal here is to tell the ATL buyers you are trying to contact the BTL and want to make sure that:

1. Larry is the right guy
2. If there are others you should reach out to
3. There is a real problem here

Follow this up with a status email after you talk to Larry (or whoever is the recommended contact), and stay with ATL early in the process.

* * *

Trumpeting Ask

Finally, the Trumpet Ask also works well, but your topic better be right on, so do your homework. Remember, ATLs really like to help.

> Dear Mary, Jane, Freda, Bill,
>
> Most companies need more quantity and quality in their lead-generation efforts and are spending too much money for too little.
>
> If you can let me know who is the appropriate person in your organization to talk with, that would be a great help.
>
> Finally, if there is a financial reason or a real issue that can be impacted, I'll send you more information.
>
> Thanks in advance,
Skip Miller
Account Manager
XYZ Company

THE REFERRAL EMAIL

In the referral email, use the name and the call to action as quick as possible. One sentence on what outcomes you may provide is about all you want to say at this point.

> Jane;
>
> Just talked with Mary Jones, and she thought we should chat. She and I were discussing what COOs are asking:
>
> 1. How can I get a head start on my 20XX objectives and avoid resource gaps?

2. What are the upcoming "invisible" market risks?
3. What can I do with increased workloads without an increase in budgets?

We provide organizations with tools that eliminate redundant fiscal tasks. I would like to spend fifteen minutes talking about your challenges and gaps for the rest of this year and the start of 20XX.

Skip

What does a prospect think of a referral email? It supplies almost instant credibility and a call to action.

▶ "Well, if Mary thought I should talk to this person, I probably should."
▶ "Mary wouldn't send me someone who wasn't worth talking to."
▶ "If Mary is telling this person to call me, I should probably take it myself."

You really can't do better than this for an introduction. Additionally, you can use a name that you don't know, just refer to it, but make sure the name is someone your prospect knows.

Jane,

Mary Jones, who I'm sure you know, had some interesting thoughts the other day. In her web event, she commented that now more than ever, COOs are asking:

• How can I get a jump on my 20XX objectives and avoid resource gaps?
• What are the upcoming "invisible" market risks?

- What can I do with increased workloads without an increase in budgets?

We provide tools to organizations that eliminate redundant fiscal tasks and would like to spend fifteen minutes talking about your upcoming challenges and gaps in these areas.

Skip

Again, tailor this for the situation and the person/title you are outbounding to. Referrals are highly leverageable and should be an early part of your outbound cadence.

THE SOCIAL EMAIL

Social email first touch should be short and brief. Of course, on LinkedIn, you should get accepted. A message like this works pretty well.

Dan,

Saw on your endorsements list that you know some people at Google. I have a few contacts there as well. Thought we should connect.

Mary

These two examples use referral statements. When you access the prospects on the LinkedIn website, look under contacts or under skills and endorsements. Most people have quite a few endorsements, and there are usually some from a company where you know folks that the prospect may know as well.

> Beth, I noticed we share mutual connections, and I just had a chance to check out (your company). It left a strong impression on me. I'd love to have you in my network.

There are other ways of connecting, but unless you have a strong LinkedIn page, successfully asking for a connect without a message—especially to an ATL—is rare.

After the connection, you want to keep in touch. Don't rush it, give it a few days. Here are a few good first-touch emails.

> Hi, John,
>
> It's been a few days since we connected, and thanks again. Wanted to give you a quick heads up that I use LinkedIn for networking and ping my connections every so often just to stay current. I'm not going to sell you on the "stuff" I do. Really.
>   Have a great morning!

> Hi, John,
>
> Thx for the connection. I'll stay in touch if something comes up that may interest you.

Remember, these are first touches. Give it week or so, then follow up, usually in conjunction with the buyer's calendar.

THE EMAILS FOR EVERY OCCASION

Here are a few emails that may help you in your cadences. First, the mail you send when they answered some of your touches but then went dark. Good for prospects who have downloaded a white paper or trial, but have not been heard from since.

The ABC Email

The ABC email is to get ahold of someone who has gone dark. This is typically used after an initial contact, so there is some rapport, but not always. It usually has a very high rate of return and usually within twenty-four hours.

This appeals to mobile device users. Instead of having to craft an entire email in response, you can just hit respond, and then say A, B, or C. Usually the response is A or B, but if it's C, at least you know it's dead for now.

Also, the humor of the C answer is optional, but it does loosen things up.

> Jim,
>
> I haven't heard from you in a while and need a favor. So I can "take a hint," can you please respond with:
>
> A: I've been busy, but I'll get back to you ASAP.
> B: Snags with the project—hang on and I'll get to you soon.
> C: I've been abducted by aliens, and we are going in a different direction. Thanks, but not now.
>
> That would help. A, B, or C please.
>
> Thanks.

The Status Email

The status email is a great way to keep the ATL in the loop while you are prospecting and trying to see if this will become a rea deal. ATLs love status emails—they get updated and don't have to follow up or do anything.

If done right, the BTLs mentioned in the status email should be all right with this, since it tells their boss they are doing a great job.

Always cc anyone mentioned in the email. Going around someone's back usually comes back to bite you.

If BTLs have a problem with the status email, explain to them the two value propositions. It's your job to make sure you hit as many trains as you can for the investment being made. If they still object, you have a choice: Let the BTLs run the sale, or deem this a lead that will never go anywhere. Your choice.

Mr. Smith,

Update to successful meeting—for your review. We had a great meeting with Lori Jones and John Thomas this week. We discussed:

ABC ROY 20XX objectives and gaps—two major issues came out of this one.

ABC competitive risks—there are three that still need to be addressed.

ABC strategies and challenges—the lack of a concrete ROI-based strategy is holding you back.

This was an exciting meeting. Our next step is to get back to Jill with some ideas quickly so you can implement them for a positive effect in 20XX.

Again, just wanted to keep you in the loop.

Regards.

● ● ●

THE BREAK-UP EMAIL

Use the break up email as a final try to get their attention.

Lucy,

I have been trying to get in touch with you regarding your interest in XXXX, and I'm sorry that we've yet to connect. We do not intend to pester or be a nuisance of any kind. That said, I'm going to close the evaluation and not ping you again. We very much appreciate you taking the time and having the interest in XXXX.

If I misconstrued our inability to get in touch as a lack of interest, please let me know. I would be more than happy to work with you and align what we do with your goals, if there is anything we can do to help you shine.

Best.

Again, tailor all these email samples to suit your style and occasion.

CHAPTER 16

Even More

The average B2B prospect gets more than fifty prospecting emails every day and takes less than two minutes to delete them. You have to get through the noise.

NOW THAT YOU have made first contact with the prospect in your outbounding efforts, how should you craft your second and third emails?

THE SECOND AND THIRD EMAILS

Your strategy for your follow-up emails in your cadence can vary widely depending on whom you are trying to contact, what time of the business year it is, and your topics. Here is a sample of a quick overall strategy that you could play out in your cadence.

QUICK STRATEGY FOR EMAIL CADENCE

Trumpet

Follow-up #1

Sorry I missed you—It's important we talk

- Issue 1—Hot topic issue
- Issue 2—Hot topic issue

I'll contact you x

Follow-up #2

Sorry I missed you
I'll contact you x

Follow-up #3

- Reason #1
- Reason #2

I'll follow up x

Follow-up #4

I am the person
As you look at 20XX+
Who is from your standpoint?
ABC Email

Follow-up #1

Dear Paul,

Very quickly, I'm Skip Miller with XYZ. I've been trying to contact you.

CXOs have been asking us recently:

What are the trends in tech I'm missing to lower costs?

What is "hot" that my team has not looked into due to lack of time and resources?

The rest of 20XX is looking very optimistic on many fronts. Would like to spend fifteen minutes talking with you about what we see as a strong competitive advantage you may be missing.

Regards,
Skip Miller
Account Manager
XYZ Company

Follow-up #2

Dear Paul,

I've been trying to contact you.

After doing some homework on your company and industry, there is probably a good reason to talk. Wasted resources can mean lack of revenue. Leads matter.

The next few months are crucial to make goals, and there are tools out there that can be implemented in a matter of days.

I'll keep trying.

Regards,
Skip Miller
Account Manager
XYZ Company

Follow-up #3

Dear Paul,

Sorry I missed you. You've been hard to get ahold of and will keep trying, but if there is a good time in the next few days, just shoot me a day to schedule a brief chat. Expect a follow up this Thursday.

Regards,
Skip Miller
Account Manager
XYZ Company

Follow-up Email #4a

Dear Paul,

Skip Miller with XYZ here. I am the person here at XYZ to make sure your company is taking the next step in using cloud networking services for 20XX.

Who in your company is chartered to look at using cloud networks and the results that companies like yours expect and actually get?

A quick direction would be much appreciated.

Regards,
Skip Miller
Account Manager
XYZ Company

Another #4a

John,

I don't know if you saw this article that appeared today in the *Wall Street Journal*. It's related to the issue I'm trying to get ahold of you about.
(Article Link)
Hope to talk soon,

Skip Miller
Account Manager
XYZ Company

Follow-up #4b

Dear Paul,

Sorry I missed you. FYI, I'm the person who will work with you and your company to see how you may be missing revenue opportunities.

Knowing that you are busy, who in your organization would be chartered to look at marketing tools that qualify leads and increase open rates? If your goals for this year are challenging, we might be able to show you a few things.

If there is a good time in the next few days, I'll be happy to schedule. Just shoot me a date.

Regards,
Skip Miller
Account Manager
XYZ Company

Here is another sample of second, third, and beyond emails. This one does a good job of referencing past and future contacts.

First Email

Hi [NAME],

There looks to be a strong alignment with your services and new challenges in the market.

Would appreciate the opportunity to discuss [COMPANY] direction and initiatives for 20XX and how these challenges can impact your thinking. Topics to possibly include are market influence, brand awareness, lead generation, and thought leadership.

Do you have twenty minutes for an introductory phone call this week?

Thanks!

Skip Miller
M3 Learning
Creating Sales Superstars

First Email (second version)

Hi [Name],

There looks to be a strong alignment with your products and new challenges in the market for 20XX.

Let's jump on an introductory call to learn about how you view these and discuss the ways companies like yours are figuring out how to tackle these head-on and drive growth and awareness in the 20XX market.

How does your schedule look this week for a
fifteen-minute call?
   Thanks!

Skip Miller
M3 Learning
Creating Sales Superstars

First Email for End of Year

Hi [Name],

I understand you may be going through budgeting right
now, and would like to set up a call to discuss how strategic
insights can fit into your plans for 20XX.
   With many companies like [COMPANY], looking at
challenges in content marketing, demand generation, lead
generation, and branding, a quick conversations and update
might be helpful.
   Do you have twenty minutes for an introductory phone
call this week?
   Thanks!

Skip Miller
M3 Learning
Creating Sales Superstars

Second Email

Hi [Name],

I'm following up on my previous note. Do you have some
time this week to connect?

We are interested in learning about some of your 20XX initiatives and gaps to see if there are some areas in which we could assist.

Thanks!

Skip Miller
M3 Learning
Creating Sales Superstars

Third Email

Hi [Name],

Following up, any thoughts? 20XX plans should be interesting and challenging for most companies, especially as they align with budgets and assets. There are a few trends out there you may want to think about.

How does your schedule look this week?

Thanks!

Skip Miller
M3 Learning
Creating Sales Superstars

Fourth Email

Hi [Name],

Following up, still looking to set up a call to discuss your initiatives for 20XX.

How does your schedule look Monday or Tuesday?

Thanks!

Skip Miller
M3 Learning
Creating Sales Superstars

Fifth Email

Hi [Name],

Following up, do you have time for a twenty-minute call this week? 20XX is just around the corner.
Thanks!

Sixth Email

Hi [Name],

Following up, any thoughts? I'm open tomorrow and Friday for a quick chat.
Thanks!

Skip Miller
M3 Learning
Creating Sales Superstars

Seventh Email

Hi [Name],

This is my last try to get in touch with you. You've outlasted me!
A call to discuss your initiatives and gaps for 20XX might be very beneficial for [COMPANY], since you are operating in a space that we are working heavily in.
How does your schedule look for a call this week?
Thanks!

Skip Miller
M3 Learning
Creating Sales Superstars

These are good since they are short, can be easily read on a mobile device, and the name and company name and tag at the end says it all, no need to talk about the dog too much.

Please tailor these to your own situation. AB test different messages based on persona and industry. Bottom line, don't talk about the dog, keep them short, and focus on outcomes.

CHAPTER 17

The Phone Call

Forty-five percent of salespeople said the phone is the most effective sales tool at their disposal.

Phone Call (fəunˌkcˑl)—A telephone call is a connection over a telephone network between the called party and the calling party.

"IF YOU WANT something done right, you need to do it yourself."

Do you remember your mother saying this? Maybe it was out of frustration, because you didn't do something right, or maybe it was her giving you some sage advice.

"If you want to outbound effectively, you have to use the phone."

• • •

HERE'S WHY YOU ARE CALLING THEM

You can stop reading this book right now if you disagree. As much as you fear the person on the other end of the line saying "Hello?" and then you getting tied up in words, having to overcome a fear of rejection, and then having the other person on the phone offer up an objection you have been trained to handle and you can't, then getting hung up on and feeling like a loser, you have to use the phone.

Look at the definition of the phrase phone call—a connection. Stop right there. A connection. Isn't that what you're really looking for, an outbounding connection to your prospect? Now that a great connection method stares you in the face, you would rather type an email, hit send, and wait for a reply?

Sure, if you get through spam filters and the thousands of other emails the prospect is getting, you might get lucky. When the other person on the connection says "Hello," you're on. You have your connection. Now what? Read on.

There is no script, no AI device, no manager who can coach you to be instantly good at outbounding using the phone. It takes practice. You need to:

1. Understand why you are calling them.
2. Understand what they are expecting when they pick up the phone.
3. Plan for the first twenty seconds.
4. Be prepared for an objection.
5. Get a next step.

Now, does that seem so hard?

THE PHONE CALL   215

HERE'S WHY

Here's a test. Why are you using the phone to outbound?

A. I was told I have to.
B. It's the most effective communication device other
than in person.
C. The result of the conversation is immediate.
D. Phone calling is old school and not worth it.

Again, if you answered D, you should probably stop reading this book. You are so adept at using the phone in all other aspects of your life, but when it comes to outbounding, your skills have not been tuned yet.

You are not calling to sell them something.

You are not calling to make a commission.

You are not calling to meet your daily call quota.

You are calling so they can obtain an outcome they desire.

Be it financial, personal, or administrative, everyone you will be talking to has a goal, and most people do not have 100 percent of their goals met, which is why they will be taking your call. They have trains in the train station that need something so they can leave the train station and be productive. That's where you can help.

WHAT THEY ARE EXPECTING

You, like everyone else in business, are busy during the day. You have meetings to attend, people you need to get back to, follow-up items that can't wait, boss's requests . . . It never stops.

So, just imagine ATL buyers, who have the additional demands of running a company or running a department, and how they feel when they get a phone call they weren't expecting. You might be a knight on a white horse relative to some of their problems, but right now, at this moment when their phone is ringing, you are probably the last person they feel they can talk to. Understand their perspective.

HOW TO RUN THE FIRST TWENTY SECONDS

Knowing that when your prospect's phone rings with a call they were not expecting, they are not really keen on dropping what they are doing at this moment to start a long call with you. Nope, just doesn't happen.

When you are using the phone to outreach to others who are not expecting your call, you are asking them to do something they don't want to do. You are asking them to break concentration and start a new train of thought. Yep, you are *interrupting them* . . . and people, especially decision makers, don't like to be interrupted.

They are thinking of fifteen different things . . . a meeting they just had, meetings they are going to have, their calendar, their week's schedule, and your call comes in. They have two minutes before the next meeting, so they take the call. What should your first twenty seconds look like?

ASTRO

"Hi, Mary. My name is Skip Miller, and I'm with M3 Learning.

"The purpose for my call is I'm looking for five to ten minutes of your time max.

"The reason would be, I've read your last quarterly report and see that you are making a major investment in sales, and typically hiring and ramping new hires to develop business skills is usually a challenge.

"We recently have worked with quite a few companies scale and ramp a lot faster than they thought they could.

"Is now or this Friday for ten minutes OK with your schedule?"

This opening follows the acronym ASTRO.

▶ ATTENTION—Get their attention, use their name.
▶ STATE—Your name and company.
▶ THE PURPOSE—An outcome, action.
▶ REFRAME–Why they should give you a few minutes.
▶ OPTIONS—Next step.

1. First, get their attention. Nothing gets someone's attention better than using their name.
2. Next, state clearly who you are.
3. Then, state your purpose using words like purpose, reason, why, intent, and/or goal. These are called pattern interrupt words. Pattern interrupt words break up a person's current thoughts and actions, like getting you off the phone, and allow for the possibility of something else taking place.

The ultimate goal of pattern interrupt words is to break the current pattern (what they are thinking or doing right now or how you are interrupting them), then causing the other person to take a moment and think about their response.

When a prospect's current pattern is interrupted, the prospect is left without a next step in their thought process or behavior, and they open up to whatever next step is offered to them in the situation. They may not agree to it, but they will at least give you a few seconds of attention.

▸ "The purpose of my call . . ." *OK, what's the purpose?*
▸ "Why I'm calling . . ." *OK, why?*
▸ "The reason for my call . . ." *OK, what's the reason?*

In each of these pattern interrupts, the prospect has to stop his or her current thought process and start thinking. It creates curiosity, which is a good thing.

4. Next, state the reason. Make it about them and why they should give you ten minutes or so.
5. Next, ask for a next step.

Simple, straightforward, and easy to cover in fifteen to twenty seconds.

IMPORTANT—you just don't jump an ASTRO. Don't speed talk from beginning to end. You can use a pause to listen for a response or an objection. Look how the previous example breaks down into ASTRO.

"Hi, Mary (GET ATTENTION. USE THE PROSPECT'S NAME). My name is Skip Miller, and I'm with M3 Learning (STATE CLEARLY WHO YOU ARE).

The reason for my call is (HERE IS THE PURPOSE, THE OB-JECTIVE, THE PATTERN INTERRUPT) I'm looking for five to ten minutes of your time, max.

The purpose would be (HERE IS THE REASON WHY. YOU HAVE DONE YOUR HOMEWORK, ALL ABOUT THEM, SO THEY ARE LISTENING. CURIOSITY)

I've read your last quarterly report (VALIDATION OF HOME-WORK) and see that you are making a major investment in sales. Typically, hiring and ramping new hires to develop business skills are usually challenging (VALIDATION OF PROBLEM). (You can pause here or ask a question too.)

We helped quite a few SaaS companies scale and ramp a lot faster than they thought they could. Is now or this Friday (NEXT STEP OPTIONS) for ten minutes OK with your schedule?"

Here is another example:

"Hi, Mary. My name is Skip Miller, and I'm with XYZ Company.

The reason for my call is I'm looking for five to ten minutes of your time, max.

I've noticed your company is growing really well, congrats. Usually, with fast growth companies, quality lead generation typically doesn't keep up.

We recently worked with a few companies to help them uncover, at a lower overall cost, more high-quality leads than they thought were available.

Do you have ten minutes now or tomorrow to see if this is something you could use?"

General rules:

1. Practice, practice, practice. Use your own voice mail and hear how you sound.
2. The goal is to get a next step, not a sale.

3. Tailor to your style.
4. Twenty seconds is a long time. The shorter, the better; try not to be longer.
5. If you have a weird name like mine, say it slowly so they can understand and not just hear.

   Hi, I'm GerTwwaStsre . . . (who?)

   Who, what? It will stop their flow. Say it slowly and enunciate.

6. Try not to create too many breaks or pauses early, except after the pattern interrupt.

   The reason for my call . . . (pause) . . . is I'm looking . . .

7. You can switch the purpose and the reason around if you want to. State why you are calling them and then ask for the commitment, or the other way around. Both work. Style thing.

This is a great tool to overcome your fears of those first few seconds on the phone. State in very clear terms the reason for the call, don't talk about the dog, and get the prospect to think. Pretty good.

WHY ASTRO WORKS

1. The A and S—using their name and quickly telling them who you are will feed into their interruption

issue, but at least it clears the air and lets you be on a first name basis.

2. The T—The Purpose. This is a pattern-interrupt moment.
3. "The purpose of my call . . ."
4. "The purpose, what purpose, OK, what . . ." is what the prospect is thinking right now.
5. "The reason for my call . . . ," "Why I'm calling is . . . ." The prospects are no longer thinking about what they were doing. Words like purpose, reason, why cause the brain to think. It's a cause-and-effect response.
6. The R—The Reframe—This is the logic why they should give you a few minutes.

   Reframe the pattern interrupt to something they can relate to.

   Make it about them.

   Make it relational—relate to their title, their industry, or their geography.

   Make them curious.

7. The O—This is the ask, and make sure you have options. Also, remember, questions hijack the brain, so end with a question.

ASTRO is a great tool and should be customized for your style. Don't be stiff or simply use the example above. Use your own words, but be brief.

ALSO, ASTRO WITH HELP

A derivative of a straight ASTRO is ASTRO with help. ATL executives usually like to help. It makes them feel good.

"Hi, John. This is Skip Miller with XYZ Company, and I could use your help."

"I'm really busy. What's up?"

"John, the purpose, Reframe, Options."

The help part at the beginning of an ASTRO script can help get prospects engaged. When you ask for help and they respond with, "What's up?" they have now agreed to at least hear what you have to say.

You've hijacked the conversation, and you have their attention for at least another ten seconds. Stay with the model and get them engaged and talking about themselves.

SUMMARY

Even in this age of social media domination, the phone remains a great two-way educational device. Get past the initial objections and interruption issues, and this will be a tool you will learn can be a great part of your arsenal.

CHAPTER 18

Objection Handling

When hearing an objection, salespeople usually become defensive and start to justify the merits of their company or product. Woof.

Objection—ob·jec·tion/əb'jekSH(ə)n/—an expression or feeling of disapproval or opposition; a reason for disagreeing. Also challenge, complaint, demur, demurral, demurrer, difficulty, exception, expostulation, fuss, kick, protest, question, remonstrance, and stink.

OBJECTIONS ARE GOING to happen—yep, that's a shocker. You need to be prepared—yep, another shocker. Here are some good ideas to prepare for objections.

When you outbound, you are invariably going to hear some objections. As much as you think you are prepared for objections, they still have a way of stopping you in your tracks. These definitions of objection handling and overcoming objections are from

HubSpot (*The Ultimate Guide to Objection Handling: 40 Common Sales Objections & How to Respond*):

> Objection handling is when a prospect presents a concern about the product/service a salesperson is selling, and the salesperson responds in a way that alleviates those concerns and allows the deal to move forward. Objections are generally around price, product fit, competitors, and good, old-fashioned brush-offs.
>
> Overcome objections in sales by actively listening, repeating what you've heard, asking follow-up questions, and responding appropriately. Avoid reacting impulsively to prospect objections. Instead, listen to them, validate their concern, ask qualifying questions, and respond in a thoughtful way.

Very good definitions. Most of the answers seem to be one-off answers and don't really help you prepare for your outbounding efforts. (For example—Question: How to overcome objections on price? Answer: Focus on value. OK, I get it, but how?)

Now, here's *how* to help you prepare for these objections.

INTERRUPTING THEM

What do you think you are doing when you reach out to a prospect, either by email, social media, or phone? You are interrupting them. Do people like to be interrupted? Clue: Not many.

So, just be prepared when you are reaching out in email and social media. The first ten to fourteen words are going to speak volumes whether the prospect is going to read or listen to the rest of your message. You're interrupting them, and they will decide within eight seconds (average human attention span) if they will be OK with being interrupted or not.

On the phone, same thing. You are interrupting them, and within the first minute, you will hear an objection:

"I'm busy right now."—If so, why did they answer the phone from a number they don't know?

"Now is not the right time."—If you can save them $1 million a month, could they find the time?

"We are happy with what we have."—Great, but will it meet the needs and changes they need to make in the next 6–12 months?

There are, of course, many more, so when you hear these or others, what should you do?

THE RIVER

When you are interrupting someone, you are really putting them in a defensive position. Research shows: If your job is to get things done and then the phone rings, it often prevents you from getting those things done, and you can even feel a sense of being harassed, regardless of the content of the phone call. Emails and social interruptions are not as bad, but still, no one likes to wake up to a bunch of spam, especially if it is a spam LinkedIn message.

When you counter an objection, here's an idea. Flow with the River. Yep, Flow with the River.

When a river flows, it gathers more oxygen. Rivers are constantly changing, carving, and evolving. If you think about it, rivers are really good at navigating obstacles quickly and efficiently along their path. They learn as they flow.

Do the same with objections. Agree with them. The prospect will feel heard, their anger and defensiveness will go down a few notches, and you then can go back and have a conversation.

Prospect: "John, I'm really busy right now."

Salesperson: "Mary, you're right, everyone is busy this time of year. Really though, what we have found is . . ."

Prospect: "Sue, this is nothing we have in the budget."

Salesperson: "Bart, I totally understand, most people we talk with about this at first never budget for something like this, however . . ."

Prospect: "Dave, thanks, but what we have is working fine."

Salesperson: "Cindy, you are right, we hear that a lot. What we also find out, though, is that as customers look at what they need for the upcoming months, they find gaps . . ."

If you agree with the customer up front, the argumentative nature of an objection is neutralized, and you then can proceed to create some curiosity or ask some questions to continue the conversation.

A quick note: It's rare you would want to take an objection head-on. It will make the other person feel less heard. However, you can do it to create a double take.

Prospect: "John, this is not a good time right now."

Salesperson: "Mary, yes, it is."

The prospect can either feel your strength and might want to know why you feel so confident, or the prospect may think you are a pompous salesperson and just end the conversation. It can be done, but flowing with the river seems to get better responses.

FEEL, FELT, FOUND

The "Feel, Felt, Found" technique is a classic objection-handling technique that most salespeople have heard. But how well you use it could make the difference between it working as intended to effectively neutralize the objection in the customer's mind and move on from it, or alternatively coming across as patronizing and increasing resistance still further.

The Process

1. First, empathize, telling prospects that you understand how they feel.
2. Then tell them about somebody who felt the same way. This builds rapport.
3. Then tell them how that other person (which should have some commonality to the person to whom you are talking) found that what they were doing was OK, but it was limiting them and postponing a new and better way.

In Practice

▸ "I understand how you feel." This wording lets prospects know that you hear them.
▸ "Others have felt (CIOs, CMOs, systems managers) the same way." You are letting prospects know that what they are thinking is a shared thought among others.
▸ "What others have found, though, was that after doing (what you want them to do) that (new outcome) was really obtainable."

Examples

> ▶ I understand how you feel about that. Many other small business owners we talk to have felt the same way. And what they have found is . . .

> ▶ I know you feel that it looks like this would be a big change. We had a customer just like you from your same state, California, who felt the same when they first started talking about it. But when they tried it, what they found in the first few weeks was a way to cut 50 percent of the time they usually would have taken to do the same thing.

> ▶ You know I feel the same about new stuff when I first think about it. I felt the same recently when I bought a new e-bicycle. I thought I didn't need it, but when I went on a demo ride with it, what I found was that I could use this more than I could imagine, because I won't have to think about whether I have enough energy to get home.

Why It Works

By empathizing with how people feel, you are building rapport with them. They feel heard, and that is a big first step to starting a conversation.

When you talk about how somebody else felt, you are actually becoming more objective. You are moving into a neutral perspective. You can see both sides, identifying the forest from the trees. Because of this perspective shift, the "my opinion vs your opinion" battle is minimized.

Additionally, it makes prospects feel like their opinion is substantiated since other people feel the same way. This herd mentality is part of our nature. We want to be accepted by others.

When you tell prospects what others in the herd have found, you then have attached them to the herd, they feel part of the herd, and since others in the herd have changed their minds, they should be open to it, too.

The Feel, Felt, Found technique is a proven strategy to get your prospects to potentially move to a new way of thinking.

FOUR NO'S

We first attacked the Four No's in *Knock Your Socks Off Prospecting.* Here is an overview.

When a prospect or a suspect says "no"—to an appointment, to a callback, or to the next step you suggest at the end of a cold call, as discussed in the previous chapter—it's important to know which No you are dealing with.

What Are the Four No's:

1. No Trust. The prospect may have a need, but something about you, your approach, or your proposal has led him or her to feel that you can't meet the need. The prospect doesn't trust you and/or your company to do what you say you will.
2. No Need. You may not be speaking to a legitimate need. If that's the case, you aren't talking to a real prospect, so move on. But it also may be that you have not sold the prospect on the idea that he has a need— even though you're convinced the need is there.
3. No Help. Sometimes there is a legitimate, important need to be met and the prospect knows it. But something about your proposal or your company or

your call feels "off." The prospect doesn't see your proposition or product working the wonders you're promising.

4. No Energy. There is a need, you have a good idea, and it probably will work. But what's the rush? Somehow, you and the prospect don't see eye to eye on the urgency of doing something. The prospect lacks energy.

KNOW YOUR NO'S WHEN YOU SEE THEM

The "No Trust" No: Signs and Symptoms of No Trust:

▸ "I would have to know more about you folks."
▸ "That's a pretty big claim."
▸ "I've never heard of you."
▸ "I'm pretty happy with who we are doing business with today (even though I don't have a clue why)."
▸ "I don't really know."—Just about anything that puts the prospect in the "I don't know you and you have not earned the right yet to take up more of my time" mode—yep, it's a trust thing.

The "No Need" No: Five Signs of Denial or a "No Need" Stall

When you hear one of these five statements from a prospect, it's even money they haven't actually evaluated their need lately. Or, if they have, they don't want you to make life complicated by forcing them to act on the need.

▸ "We're happy with what we have."

▸ "We're not in the market just now."

▸ "We aren't ready for an upgrade."

▸ "We haven't gotten all the value out of the Acme 4000."

▸ "It is not a priority for me right now (even though the holes in the dam are getting bigger, and the flood is coming)."

Any of these forms of No should prompt you to continue probing.

The "No Help" No: Symptoms of a "No Help" No

You and the prospect are probably in the No Help tango when you hear phrases like these:

▸ "We would never need anything this complicated."

▸ "I don't see how your product meets a need for us."

▸ "We already do business with someone who can do that."

Getting a prospect to talk here requires you to focus on a solution the buyer can see. Ask, "What could our product do better?" or, "How do you see your needs changing over the next year in this area?" You need to move the prospect off his or her current center. If you are not the lead dog on a dog sled, the view never changes, but the starting point has been left behind a long time ago.

The "No Energy" No: Sounds of the "No Energy" No

The "No Energy" No is probably at the root of an appointment or callback or next-step refusal when you hear things like:

▸ "We'll need to do that eventually, but . . ."

- ▸ "I'm sure that when we really need to do that, you'll be on our list."
- ▸ "If you'd like to send me something, we'll keep it on file."
- ▸ "We're just not ready to . . . ."
- ▸ "I'll get back to you when . . ."

To counter this one, recognize that the real issue is change. Change is inevitable, but no one likes to change. Here is where you ask about changes the prospect is facing and gain agreement that there is a need to change faster than the prospect thinks. He or she is stuck in neutral on the tracks of change and don't see that train coming.

Plan to hear the Four No's throughout the prospecting process and be ready for them—especially at the end of a cold call. If there is a No at the end of the call, it most likely will be one of these four.

CHAPTER 19

Personal Habits to Overcome Objections

An objection is better than a "no"; it gives you a place to begin a conversation. Here are some good personal tips and best practices that can help you.

WHEN DOING HOMEWORK, you run across some great ideas. I saw these following thoughts from a Gong.io study, some HubSpot stuff, and got some really cool info from a customer, thanks John, and thought they were important.

1. PAUSE, SPEAK WITH CALM AUTHORITY

Successful reps pause after objections. In fact, they pause for longer after an objection than during other parts of a sales call.

Unsuccessful reps often interrupt the customer upon receiving an objection. They pounce on objections, getting "all fired up." They also speak faster after hearing an objection. It's as if objections make them nervous.

Top producers slow it down. Maintain a calm demeanor amid a flurry of objections, and you'll build trust with your customer.

2. CLARIFY WITH QUESTIONS

Successful salespeople respond to objections with a question. Objection scenarios are rife with potential misunderstandings. If you don't clarify them, you might address the wrong issue. Doing so creates friction. Now, here's what low performers do instead: They react with a knee-jerk monologue.

Ask a help question you can use to clarify objections.

"Can you help me understand what's causing that concern?"

Notice that this question asks "why" without uttering the word *why*. Overcoming an objection is like peeling an onion. The core of the onion is what you want to address. You have to peel back the outer layers.

3. VALIDATE THE OBJECTION

Did you know that humans go through 95 percent of their lives feeling misunderstood? If you are the person who understands them, you'll carry powerful influence. Help them feel they have been heard: "I hear you," or, "I can really see where you are coming from on this. . . ."

4. ADDRESS WITH A "180"

Use 180 statements to get your buyer to see things through a new lens. Here's an example: If you try to get your buyers to trial your software, an objection you might often face is: "I don't want to start a trial until after next month. We're too busy closing out the quarter. Right now is the worst time to for us to do this."

You can 180 that objection from "bad timing" to "perfect timing."

"John, really, this is a perfect time for you to start a trial. You probably have all the work done on what you have to do for the quarter, and you and a few others have to push it across the finish line. Your employees who brought everything to the finish line are done and are waiting to get started on next quarter. Let me go talk to Mary and Fred, it won't take up too much of their time, and we will develop a game plan so when the quarter does end, you'll be in a great position to make a decision early in the next quarter and get a head start."

Stumped at coming up with your own 180s? Think of a common objection you're currently struggling with.

Got it? Now ask these questions about it: Is the objection:

▸ A problem that can be 180'd into an opportunity?
▸ A weakness that can be 180'd into a strength?
▸ Poor timing that can be 180'd into perfect timing?
▸ Too risky that can be 180'd into a certainty?

Ask those questions, and you'll come up with some great 180s. These are great ideas to help calm yourself down and be mentally and physically prepared to handle objections.

●　※　◦

IT'S NOT ABOUT YOU

Dealing with rejection is not the easiest thing to overcome. When the success rate is one or two out of ten, that's a whole lot of rejections that pile up.

The normal cop out is when you start blaming others or blaming yourself: "I'm having a bad day." "No one seems to be interested." "I'm reaching jerk central today."

After each live rejection, go over your how-to-handle-objections process and see what you might have done better. Remember, two out of ten is pretty good, but you have to get past the other eight.

To control your emotions and not take outbounding rejections personally are learned skills. You are not born with them. No one likes rejection, and you need to remember this is business, it's not personal. Usually the problem is with the other person.

Breathe and remember that this is not about you. Business is business, so when an objection comes up, seeking to understand may be a better idea than getting defensive.

ASK ENGAGING QUESTIONS

Sales actually require more listening than talking. A lot more. Once you begin your conversation with a prospect, it's important to listen intently to what his or her current problems are and how you can help fix them. Talking about your dog here is not a good idea.

Listen carefully to any hesitation they may have and call it out. It will get them to start talking.

"Jim, I sense some hesitancy in your response. What's up?"

Objections are usually quite high level, so bringing them down from 30,000 feet to, say, about 5,000 feet would be another good tactic.

"Mary, you said to call in sixty days. I have a feeling if we chat for five minutes, you'll start to see how much time and money you may be wasting if you delay for sixty days."

CREATE A SAMPLE OF FIVE TO SEVEN COMMON OBJECTIONS YOU HEAR

You want to have a list of some of the most common objections you hear, and some pointers on where you can start. Having a paragraph after the objection will come off like you are reading something. Also, by the time you have read how you should respond, the prospect probably has hung up. Create that list so you don't have to think on your feet, also called dancing.

1. "Just send me some information."—What type of information/break into threes.

    This is a great good/better/best tactic, and the power of threes is well known.

    "I'll be happy to do that. We have three types of information. The financial ROI, the How to Use, and How Others Have Used Successfully. Which one would be helpful for you?" Make them think.

2. "Call me back next quarter."—Agree/offer mid-step/different step

    Of course, always agree with the objection, but gain control back and offer a mid-step.

    "Happy to do that, but if we can spend five minutes right now, that will make next quarter go really well."

    "Happy to, but what is so special about next quarter?"—Uncover real objection, like "I'm too busy."

3. "Does your product do X, Y, and Z?"—Agree/flip/define

"Thank you for asking. It does quite a few things. If I could ask, what's the outcome you would want if it did these things?"

4. "We already work with [competitor]."—Time travel

"Fully understand (PAST). Have there been things going on the last few months that if you could change it you would?"

"Fully understand (FUTURE). Quick question then: If you look down the next three to six months, what different things are coming that will make you do things differently, like an increase in costs or new competitive offerings?"

5. "We don't have the budget . . ."—Outcomes solve problems

"I appreciate that. What we usually find is when we have a quick discussion on gaps and problems and talk about desired outcomes and how those may be attained, finding the budget is not a huge problem."

6. "Sorry, now's a bad time."—Agree, go for 24/48 hours and five minutes

"So sorry, I fully agree. When this afternoon or tomorrow morning would be a better time? I promise five minutes, that's it." (Make sure they think about it or really agree to the time you throw out) "OK, today at 4:00. Perfect, and you're sure you don't have anything scheduled. I can wait while you check."

7. "Can you call me back next week?"—Schedule/
   challenge
   "Happy to, did you want to look at your calendar
   and see what will work for you? I can wait."
   "Happy to, but a quick question. Are you saying
   next week or do you mean never? I really believe,
   based on my homework, it will be worth five minutes
   of your time."
   Build a list and keep it next to your desk for a quick
   reference.

▶ My Objections List

---

1. "Just send me some information."–What type of
   information/break into threes
2. "Call me back next quarter."–Agree/offer mid-step/
   different step
3. "Does your product do X, Y, and Z?"–Agree/flip/define
4. "We already work with [competitor]."–Time travel
5. "We don't have the budget."–Outcomes solve problems
6. "Sorry, now's a bad time."–Agree, go for 24/48 hours
   and five minutes
7. "Can you call me back next week?"–Schedule/challenge

GET A NEXT STEP

You are not selling anything yet. Your job when you get them on
the phone is to sell them a next step.

This is a first date, not a let's-go-to-the-jewelry-store-and-pick-out-a-ring moment. Salespeople are so nervous, they want to blurt out what they do and hope something sticks.

"If I can get what's in my head in their head, they'd see why they should buy from me."

"I've got to get them interested in what we do to see if there's a fit!"

"Once I tell them who we are and what we do, we can go from there."

Wrong! The goal of your first contact is to get a second contact. Options for this are:

1. ATL Education—You need to know more about goals and outcomes and gaps for the next six to twelve months. You need to hunt for trains in the ATL train station.
2. BTL Education—You need to get some information on what the BTL is doing and how you might do it better, then get back to the ATL with some recommendations.
3. ATL Validation—Have a discussion on specific outcomes (identified trains) the ATL wants for the investments being made in the next three to twelve months, and then provide information on how you can help do that. This is very different from ATL Education.

There are more; define them. Don't wing the next step. It will give the impression that you don't know what you are doing, and the client will then take over the sales process.

Here are terrible next steps:

1. A presentation—Really? I get to sit through thirty slides that are all about you?

2. A demonstration (demo)—Really? I get to see how the printer prints? How a car engine works? For the BTL, sure, make it short, and then get information. A product rarely sells itself.

3. A meeting—For what? Always out the action first. "A good next step should be a discussion about next year's goals and challenges. Let's set a meeting for that this Friday." Never, "Let's set a meeting for this Friday to discuss. . . ." You lost them at the mention of the word *meeting*. They hate meetings.

MESSAGE GUIDELINES

Bottom line, outside of a brief overview to set the stage, less than a minute, *no woofing*. It's not about the dog, yet. Save that for the next couple of steps. The best thing you can have after the first call is the prospect going: "They heard me. They know what we are trying to do. They heard me."

If you hang up the phone thinking: "They really get what we are trying to do. We really got our points across!" you may want to rethink your strategy. It's not about you . . . yet.

FOCUS ON OUTCOMES

After that first call, you should be able to write down what change the prospect is trying to accomplish and by how much.

"I need a 40 percent improvement in our lead generation process."

"I have to have a 50 percent growth in revenue, and I only see about half of that."

"I'm tired of working sixty hours per week. I have to get back to the normal forty hours a week like everyone else."

ATL and BTL will have different agendas, and that's great. Try to get multiple trains and quantified cause for change, not quantified cause to buy your stuff.

That's it. What and how to make that first call and get their interest. So, now they say, "OK, you got five minutes. What's up?" What should you do? Great next-step lead-ins coming up.

CHAPTER 20

Lead-ins and Voice Mails

Sixty percent of inbound leads want to discuss pricing on the first call. Less than 10 percent on the first outbound. Be prepared.

YOU NOW HAVE your first fifteen to twenty seconds down pat. The prospect has signaled that he or she wants to hear more. OK, now what?

Here are a couple of good next-step lead-ins once the prospect is curious enough to take some time and hear you out.

A lead-in is a direction you want the conversation to go, so you *lead into* the conversation with intention. It gives you a plan for how to take the conversation once you and the prospect have decided to spend a little time together.

If the prospect agrees to give you some time:

"So, what's this about?"

"I have two minutes. What's up?"

"OK, what do you need from me?"

The last thing you want to do is blow prospects over with all your stuff. Woof. You want to get them to talk more about why they are giving you a few minutes and give them a reason and a direction to talk.

LEAD-IN IDEAS

Cause Lead-In: "As you look at next quarter, what would cause you to think about making a change?"

Remember, people hate to change, and now they are considering making a change, and it's fearful and they want to talk about it.

Direction Lead-In: "Who in your organization/company would be chartered to look at . . ."

It's a great way to get an ATL to delegate to a BTL, but remember not to let go of the ATL.

"OK, I'll contact Bob, thanks. If all goes well talking with him, I may have a few questions for you and future outcomes for this kind of investment."

Time Travel Lead-In: "As you look at the next few months . . ."

This is a great tool for ATLs. It's where they live. It's the topic for their next twenty-five meetings.

Relate Lead-In: "I've talked to several CMOs in the past few weeks, and their questions are all kind of similar . . ."

Lead-ins are for getting ATLs to discuss what they think about their industry and others. It makes them feel important. It also could be where the ATL says, "It's not important to me what everyone else does." Be ready for that. Double down, time travel, and say:

"OK, sorry about that. As you look to the next few months, what unique questions *are* on your desk?"

The Time Travel Lead-In is usually a good tool to get someone off their current pedestal and get them to start thinking and talking.

Lead-ins can also be questions based on your homework.

"I noticed in your annual report you are planning to grow 100 percent over the next twelve months. What do you see as your biggest challenges?"

Prepare a few lead-ins so you are comfortable with starting a dialogue. Much better than "winging it."

I always find that first minute of conversation uncomfortable. If I can get past the first minute, I'm good.

VOICE MAIL

Voice mail is going to have limited use. If you expect an ATL to call you back, don't hold your breath. A BTL might, but not an ATL. Please also keep any voice mail to ten to fourteen seconds. Do not ramble.

A voice mail is, however, a touch, and it can keep momentum alive. With visual voice mail being used more, it can keep you top of mind to the prospect, and it will keep your cadences alive.

Your message should not be call me back though, because they usually don't.

Here are some suggestions:

1. Next Step message—This message just announces a next step to get the prospect ready. A little reminder that I'm trying to get ahold of you.

    "John, Skip Miller. Trying to get ahold of you for a few minutes. I'll follow up with an email in a few hours. Talk soon."

    The goal here is to keep rapport going, stay in cadence, send the message you are persistent, and at least alert the prospect that the next communication is on its way.

2. Directional message—This is a message that instructs and gives them something to do.

    "Hi, John. Skip Miller with M3 Learning. No need to call me back, but if you can look at the email I sent you the other day. I'll send it again; there's probably a good reason for us to talk for a few minutes. Thanks for taking the time. Again, Skip with M3."

    If you tell a buyer you have sent them something, they now have been alerted to it, and they will actually spend time to hunt it down. People usually do what they are told to do. Not too heavy here, a good suggestion to look at the email I'm going to resend should prompt curiosity and allow the prospect to say, "OK, what is this?"

3. Twenty-Second Help Speech—People usually like to help. A short help speech can be very effective.

> ▶ Help Speech

"Please leave a message at the tone, and I'll get back to you as soon as I can." *Beep.*
   "Hello, Mr. Gregs. My name is Skip Miller from the XYZ Company, and I could really use your help. Please call me back at 959.123.7890."

A simple I-need-your-help speech. Here are the components:

1. Introduction—You state your name and your company. That's it. No more, no less. You do need to state your company, since just stating your name leaves the prospect wondering who it is and could be misleading. Simple and straightforward, name and company.
2. Call for help—Here is where you ask for help. Keep it simple; you want to just ask for help. Do not give a reason why you are looking for help, just ask for it. You will be surprised how many ATL executives want to help.
3. Request action—Tell the prospect where to call you back.

That's it. Pretty simple. Here's why this works.

1. There are many people who want to help if your request is sincere.
2. Do not add what you do or any other information; keep to the script.

3. Be honest; really ask for help.
4. When the prospect calls you back, just ask for directions. Yes, ask for directions.

"This is Ken Gregs returning your call."

"Yes, Mr. Gregs, thanks for the callback. The reason I called was my company, XXXX, helps companies reduce the burden of marketing lead-generation expenses and lead reporting. I could use your help in determining who in your organization would be responsible for looking into something like this?"

It's a legitimate call. You are asking for directions. You can save this company a ton of money, and if they have been looking into an issue like this, they probably should add a vendor like you to the list. If they aren't looking at this, they probably should.

It's all about their ATL value proposition. If they were looking at something that you could contribute to, why wouldn't they look at you as a piece of the puzzle?

How can something so simple be effective? We have consistently documented over the past years companies that use this twenty-second speech format have a thirty-plus percent callback ratio. Why? Again, it's because people generally want to help.

There is an addition to this speech if you want, and it's to add a referral. You can add the name only of someone who may cause rapport to be built.

"Please leave a message after the tone, and I'll get back to you as soon as I can." *Beep.*

"Hello, Mr. Gregs. My name is Skip Miller from the XYZ Company. I was talking to Deb Ricci, and I could really use your help. Please call me back at 959-555-4567."

Of course, Deb better be someone you know and someone they know. It could be a referral, a coworker, someone in the industry who has prominence that you know. Don't lie. Don't say, "I was talking to the president of your company" or something that they can easily check on.

You can make it about someone who works for them, since they will probably be curious. Just have integrity and be up front. You'll know when you have crossed the line.

CHAPTER 21

Three Levels of Why and Homework Assignments

Listening builds trust, loyalty, engagement, enthusiasm, and commitment. Leaders who are strong and connected speakers do so through their skill as good listeners. —Dale Carnegie

THREE LEVELS OF WHY

Three Levels of Why is a questioning technique that all good salespeople should master. It's also a great tool for outbounding salespeople, since you want to make sure you can tell if what the prospects are saying is what they really mean.

It's getting to the question behind the question kind of thing. It is a way for the salesperson to really understand the true needs of both ATL and BTL buyers.

There is a real reason why people make decisions. There is a real reason why you choose things. There is a real reason you wear the watch you wear, drive the car you drive, live where you live. There is a *real* reason.

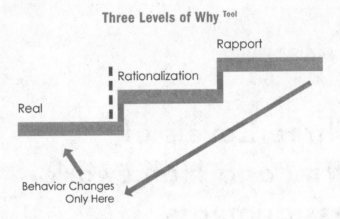

Three Levels of Why Tool

People do not like to talk about their real reasons, so they rationalize their decisions. Again, people do not like to openly discuss their rationalizations, so they develop rapport reasons to tell others why they made the choices they made. If this is true, the inverse must be true, and you can only change behavior at the Third Level of Why.

Rapport reasons are typically what salespeople get when they ask questions in a sales environment. Good salespeople get down to the second level of why. Great salespeople know to go deeper and get to the Third Level of Why.

An example of Three Levels of Why:

"That's a really nice watch you are wearing. Why did you buy that watch?"

"I liked the color. I like a watch that has gold and silver." (Rapport)

"I'm sure there were a lot of gold and silver watches. Why did you buy that watch?"

"I like the look. It is sporty, yet classic. I wanted a watch that you could wear every day, yet still would look good on special occasions." (Rationalization)

"I am sure there were many watches that were sporty yet classic. Why did you buy *that* watch?" (Real)

"You want to know why, I'll tell you exactly *why*. I just got a promotion at work, and I have always wanted this brand of watch. I bought the watch because I earned it."

This is an example of Three Levels of Why, and getting to the real reason. If you were a watch salesperson, you know why this person would buy a certain watch. You know their real reason. If you do not have the watch they are looking for, you now know the real reason why, and you can build rapport and potentially influence their behavior.

"I am sure that is a good watch, but people who just got the promotion they felt they deserved also looked at this watch here."

You now have a chance with this buyer, since you know their real level of why. How do you know when you are at the Third Level of Why? You know. The nonverbal signs, the passion, the voice inflection . . . you know when you are there. How do you get there? You ask:

Why—"Why would you do that?"

What—"What would that mean to you?"

Flip—"So, I think I hear you say this, is that correct?"

Three Levels of Why is a tool to be used when you are outbounding and asking a prospect questions about why they are making a decision, especially why they would need to make a change.

How will you know when you get to the Third Level of Why? You'll know . . . the emotion, the passion comes out. There's an emotional wall that separates the Second and Third Levels of Why. Emotions are at the Third Level of Why, and you can argue that most if not all decisions are emotional, and then they are rationalized, and then rapport answers are created.

If this is true, the inverse must be true, and an outbound salesperson who masters the Three Levels of Why to get to the real reason will get a head start on qualifying the prospect. The emotional reasons a prospect makes a decision to start talking with you is what you really want to find out when you are outbounding.

THREE LEVELS OF WHY—NEW STORY

For some reason, Three Levels of Why is one of the tools people really remember from our trainings, and we usually only get to cover it about half the time.

For outbounding salespeople and SDRs, this tool should allow you to really understand the prospect's motivation and allow you to qualify early for intent and energy.

A quick story, one of many, may help you here.

"I was just on your website, and it said to call for some more information and get the free report, so that's what I'm doing."

"Thank you for stopping by. Happy to send you the report. May I ask you why you stopped by the website and what caught your eye regarding the report?"

"Oh, it's a topic that has interested me for some time now, and I thought I'd just get some current information."

Prodding the SDR on the phone to continue, she asked, "What caused you to surf the web and hit our website today? Why the sudden interest?"

(You notice she asked about energy, the caller's intent, rather than focus on the dog, like, "So, what current information of ours do you need?")

"I find it fascinating that this area is one that has such enormous benefits, and we don't even have anything like this up and running."

"Well, that's great. Happy to send you some information. One last question, though. Why now? What's going on where it made you actually want to talk to us and get a current report now?"

His response was stunning. "Well, I just got a new boss, told him about this, and he agreed that we need to get on this as soon as we can. My old boss wouldn't listen to me for the past two years. I finally feel I've been listened to, and I'm not going to waste this chance."

Oh, yes, the emotional wall. Probably a good lead. Just sayin'.

LEFT-FIELD WORDS

There are words a prospect uses that seem to come out of left field. The term *out of left field* is used to imply that the topic or event appeared with no context. It just appeared.

Left-field words can appear when you are talking to a prospect, and you can tell the word has passion and depth to it, since it's just a bit out of place.

"I like fine *timepieces*."—Most people call them watches.

"That's an *unusual* shirt you have on."—Most people wouldn't call a shirt unusual.

"Your solution seems to be a bit *dark*."—Never heard a of solution being dark before.

These left-field words, when you hear them, are great to go Three Levels of Why on and get to the true motivation, or the real level of why.

QUALIFY AND DISQUALIFY

There probably are very few tasks an outbounding salesperson should master than qualification and disqualification skills.

▸ Qualify—The questions you ask and the things you do
   to try to keep a sales deal in the funnel.
▸ Disqualify—The questions you ask and the things you
   do to try to get a sales deal out of the funnel.

On an inbound lead, this is critical. Way too much time is wasted on deals that are going to be going nowhere, due to a lack of budget, energy, and focus. Both these efforts are important.

For an outbound lead, going back to Stage 0, it's tough to qualify or disqualify a lead when that initial interest is not there yet. It's almost like they don't know they don't know they may need something to fix a problem they don't know they have. (Whew)

HOMEWORK ASSIGNMENTS

A great way to qualify or disqualify an outbound lead is to make a homework assignment. By asking the prospect to do something or send you something, you are actually gauging their energy to want to get something done.

A homework assignment can be something as simple as asking them to send you a one-page data sheet, letting you talk to someone else and then getting back to them, or even asking them to review something you send, mark it up, and return it to you.

Anything that creates "sweat equity" can be seen as a homework assignment, and if they are willing to take some action, they usually are more qualified than most.

Caution note: This is usually not to be used with BTLs who are just kicking tires. They love getting involved and will put a ton of energy into something that has no chance of happening. Homework assignments usually work well with ATLs, since they value their time more than BTLs, and they will only do a homework assignment if they have some sort of train in the station.

Samples of Homework assignments:

▶ Send a copy of a current slide deck.
▶ Mark up an agenda for a next step and send it back.
▶ Send an invite to a subordinate asking him or her to speak to you.
▶ Have them send back to you a simple questionnaire (multiple choice, not essay!).
▶ Take a Survey Monkey or anything that requires them to give an opinion.
▶ Have them set up the next Zoom meeting on their Zoom account.
▶ Have them send you a calendar invite.
▶ Have them hop on a video call link on the first call (requires them to take some action).

There are a lot of things you can have someone do, but it needs to be useful to both parties. Just having them do something so you can get them to do it, and it really has no value kind of lacks integrity. Homework Assignments are a great way to qualify, but they really do need to be of mutual value.

SUMMARY

The tools in this chapter are great listening-skill tools. Even homework assignments will depend on you listening to your prospect and determining which homework assignment would be mutually beneficial. Most of the tools here are advanced tools, so practice, practice, practice.

CHAPTER 22

Other Types of Prospecting

HERE ARE THE top ways to create a positive sales experience, according to buyers:

- Ask and listen (69 percent).
- Provide information important to me (61 percent).
- Respond in a timely manner (51 percent).

There are many ways to outbound, some very direct, like in person and over the phone, and some indirect. Really, anything where you are trying to get your prospect's attention is outbounding. Here are some different types of outbounding.

• • •

UPSELL OUTBOUNDING

Upsell outbounding is a misleading term. Upselling implies the old McDonald's "Do you want fries with that?" approach. What it really should be called is *growth selling*.

When customers buy something, most of the time they buy to solve a problem. They usually are not thinking of other options.

1. They didn't buy for everyone. They had a problem they were willing to take one step toward solving. If what they bought goes well, they may need more over time. Other people or other department or divisions. This is usually called *land and expand*.

2. They didn't buy all they could use. They bought some golf irons, but not the woods or a putter. They may need other things that the vendor is selling over time. Most vendors have multiple products, but their customers usually start out with one, then they work with the vendor to potentially uncover more.

3. Changes. Companies change over time. Trains in the station leave and new trains enter. This is a big opportunity for outbounding efforts, and one that many people miss. They miss it because they are not looking at it correctly.

NOUN VS VERB

The changes that companies go through and the new initiatives that the ATL buyer has are usually missed by most outbounding efforts. They are not thinking about change and are thinking too statically. You cannot think of these opportunities as THE

RENEWAL, a noun. You have to put action or motion into them, and change THE RENEWAL to a verb with action.

Example: It is now the start of the fourth quarter, and John is looking for THE RENEWAL (a noun). Back in January, the ABC Company made a nice-sized purchase of John's offering, to the tune of about $200,000. It was a nice order, and since John's company sells an annual subscription, he's looking for THE RENEWAL (a noun).

Mary, the ATL buyer at ABC, and Fred, the BTL buyer, were excited back then. They liked what they bought, and John's company even made a white paper case study from what ABC was using John's services and products for. All is good.

So, for the last three quarters, John and Fred have made sure everything is working well and most people are happy. Now, start of the fourth quarter, it's time to start thinking of THE RENEWAL (noun).

"John, it's been a great year, and you and your company have done great work. However, I've been informed that we will probably get about 80 percent of this year's budget for next year, so we need to think about where we can cut some services."

"Fred, that's nuts, and you know it. You folks use the heck out of our stuff, and to cut back is really going to effect the users."

"I know, I know" Fred says, exasperated, "but I only can work with what they give me. It's belt-tightening everywhere. I feel lucky I came away with the 80 percent. So, where can we reduce some and stay within budget?"

Here's what John has missed.

• • •

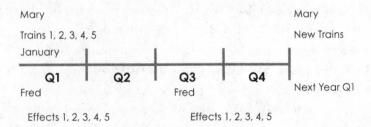

Back in January, John (BTL) had a list of needs, called effects (Cause and Effect Split) he needed to buy. Mary (ATL) had some reason or cause to also make the purchase (called trains in the train station). Both ATL and BTL buyers were aligned and the purchase was made.

Now, three quarters later, John still likes using Fred's stuff, but most of Mary's first quarter trains have left the station. She now has some new trains coming down the track for the first quarter of next year.

1. Mary's new trains probably don't link to her last year's trains. New markets, competitive pressures, and new demands on the business have given Mary a whole host of new initiatives (trains) she has to fund.

2. Mary's trains from the previous first quarter are doing well. No need to keep maximum funding on those trains—most have left the train station and are doing well.

3. John has pleaded with Mary for the $200,000 renewal, and Mary has approved 80 percent, grudgingly. She needs money to fund the new trains.

4. Mary is not relating her new trains to what John sells. John's services and new products could potentially help Mary's new trains. She just doesn't see it right now.

5. Fred is not invited to Mary's next year's executive meetings, he's not an executive, so he does not know what is coming down in the first quarter.

6. John did have a meeting with both Mary and Fred and did a good job of pitching how valuable John's stuff has been over the last three quarters and will continue to be, so he's looking for THE RENEWAL (noun).

What John should have done was treat the renewal as a verb, not a noun and not be stagnant. He should have known what he sold Fred probably wouldn't change too much, but Mary's requirements usually always change.

By justifying THE RENEWAL by looking backward, John did not focus the renewal on Mary's trains. He did not see Mary's changes (action), and therefore, he will not only lose 20 percent on THE RENEWAL, but miss a great upsell opportunity for next year, because while he was justifying the last nine months, he ignored Mary's needs for the next nine months.

Bottom line: Sell both forward and backward for renewal opportunities. Treat THE RENEWAL as a verb, not a noun.

OTHER OPTIONS

You can outbound by sending out a monthly newsletter that could be about your industry to keep people informed. The same with blogs, podcasts, and any type of social media. There always is a strong demand for content. Just make it interesting for the reader, not about you, not about the dog, and do some research. It's not really about your opinion, it's about what your prospect wants and needs to know.

Parachuting is a way to have some fun when outbounding as well. Parachuting is when you drop into someone else's territory and hunt for prospects. Since they won't be your prospects, you are a bit less emotionally attached. Calling high, asking for the ATL, objection handling, and asking for homework all gets a bit easier when you have no skin in the game.

Make an agreement with another salesperson for a half day, swap territories, and go at it. Pretty fun game and a way to overcome some of your own outbounding fears.

THE IN-PERSON MEETING

What do you do when you are meeting someone in person for a first call?

There will be opportunities for you to outbound in person, either one-on-one (door knocking), events, or actual scheduled meetings. Two-way communication increases with face-to-face interactions, so even though sending an email is easier, a face-to-face opportunity is always valuable and should not be passed up.

The "Did you want to talk on the phone or meet in person?" email, if possible, should be answered: "In person is best. When's a good time? This week works." Some inside salespeople are allowed to travel, some not. If you can, in-person is the best, as long as you maximize your time and qualify beforehand.

Some basic rules for meeting in person:

1. Dress appropriately. You don't have to be in your best clothes, but the T-shirt and sneakers you usually wear around the office are probably not the look you want to represent your company.

2. Your goal is to listen and determine if there is an opportunity. Think about what are some good next steps? Try to get a business card, or at least an email. Bring something to write with. Use 3-1-2.

3. Ask questions about their role and their business. Be curious. Be sincere.

4. Hunt for trains, ask about gaps. Time travel to get at what are the real issues, don't ask about right now. "What's going on in the next few months?" is a better question than "Why are you at this conference?"

SUMMARY

The more you use the tools for all different types of outbounding, the more complete a salesperson you will be.

CHAPTER 23

You Are Live: More Hints

Only 7 percent of top sales and SDRs report pitching their stuff on a first call, while 24 percent of lower-performing folks are recorded pitching their offering right up front. (Woof)

IT'S TIME. TIME for you to pick up the phone and make a call. Scared? This is nothing to be afraid of. With good ol' preparation and practice and an understanding of the other person on the phone, you'll be a master at using the phone. You may still not like the rude rejections you get, but learning how to use that rejection energy to your advantage will be a key to your success.

You are twice as effective in your outbound sequences if you use the phone and other forms of communication like social media and email. The phone is instant two-way communication, and only the in-person meeting has a better success rate. So, when using the phone for outbounding, which is what most of you will be using, what's the plan of attack?

PREPARE

Most of you when preparing to outbound on the phone, will do some homework on the person you are talking to, then dial, then if lucky enough, get someone on the phone to say, "Hello?" What do you do then, hang up?

Being prepared is really thinking about the other person on the phone as well. Some general rules to remember:

1. As discussed before, the person taking your call is being interrupted by your call. Hey, people hate to be interrupted. You are starting off on the wrong foot.
2. The prospect you are calling has chosen to take your call and say, "Hello?" By doing so, you know they have a spare second or two. They would have let your call go to voice mail if they were in the middle of something.
3. When they accept a call, they can see on their phone it's a number they don't know. They are taking the call because they are curious. Use this to your advantage.
4. Knowing they have a free moment, and you are interrupting them, you have to change their state, from interruption to curious, if you want them to start to listen.
5. The goal of this call is not to sell anything. The goal is to get to an agreed next step, which could be now or later.

DIRECTION

There are some basic steps and directional goals you want to have in mind before you start.

1. Establish rapport: You shouldn't shy away from personal conversations. A great way to start is by using their name, and then follow up using your homework.
    "Hi, John. Skip Miller from M3 here."
2. Hunt for trains: Dive into their pain points/trains during the call if ATL, and find out what their current problems are if BTL.
    "What's causing you to make a change to your marketing platform?"
3. Identify gaps: Ask questions about the business. Get numbers. The train is in the station for a reason.
    "What's the size of this problem?"
4. Wrap it up: Find a calendar time between twenty-four and forty-eight hours.
    "Would you have fifteen or twenty minutes to follow up this week? My colleague, John, will join us—he's an expert in this area. What works best for you?"
5. Change their state: We are usually in an internal mental state. You call someone on the phone, and they answer to a number they don't know, they are thinking, what's this about and do I need to stay on this call? An internal state of mind fluctuates between thinking and engaged, and to get them to engage you must interrupt their current state, to an external state, one of curiosity about you and what you are going say.

PATTERN INTERRUPTS

A pattern interrupt is an important tool in outbounding. Here's some more information on it so you can really understand its importance.

What is a pattern interrupt? Anything that interrupts a pattern. It's a technique to change a particular thought, behavior, or situation. Behavioral psychology uses this technique to interrupt and change thought patterns and behaviors.

We have an average of up to fifty thousand thoughts per day. Up to 95 percent are the same thoughts, repeated every day. That's a lot of repetition and patterns you fall into. You need to break the pattern of the person answering the phone and who immediately wants to get off the phone, which is a pattern.

"I don't know this person; there is nothing in it for me (Internal), so I need to get off the phone."

You need to break this pattern with an interrupt. Here are some tools for you to work with.

CAUSE

Here is the big mix-up. You are thinking what would cause them to talk to me, which is all about you, so that's not the right attitude to think.

What is causing them to pick up the phone and take your call? They did it for a reason. Also, since businesses are always changing, and change is something people usually don't like to do, and they usually don't have all the answers (risks), this is the playground you should be playing on.

Do your homework with this question on our brain.

"What is compelling them to make a change?"

You'll pick up a ton of good ideas for your ASTRO pitch.

Why is their stock price down?

Why is she in this position for only three months? What happened, good or bad?

What are the expectations from their last quarterly report and how are they doing against them?

The industry trends are out there by a ton of experts. How are they prepared for these changes?

Do your homework for changes and what is causing those changes. All about them, right? Being able to relate to a feeling or experience means that you understand it. It might mean that you've had the same feeling or experience before. In other words, this is an opportunity to show sympathy, and it helps build rapport.

NEXT STEPS AND OPTIONS

Most salespeople freeze after their ASTRO speech because they weren't prepared for a next step, or they get an objection. Lead-ins will provide that needed direction so you can head off the objections.

Objections

Objections like the Four No's and Flow with the River have been covered already. Some common objections can be classified into:

Not Me—You have the wrong person.

Not Now—Bad timing. I'm busy right now, or we are taking that up next year.

Not Never—Rarely true. You usually sell something that is unique, and they may be happy with what they have, but business is always changing.

Talk Now

The goal is to have an immediate next step, which would be to talk right now. If they can't talk now, set up a call within forty-eight hours, three days max. Ask them for an email address so you can send them an invitation.

Who Else Should I Talk With?

The goal is to talk about an issue or problem. ATL buyers love to delegate. Just make sure to remind them, if you accept the person they send you to, that you will be following up with them later.

"Thanks, John. I'll follow up with Harry, and if there's a reason to get back in touch with you and get some clarification, I'll call you then."

Start the Buy/Sell Process

If the call goes well, being a directional and intentional salesperson, you now can launch into a buy/sales process. This journey can take ten minutes, three months, or a year, but making sure you and the customer take each next step together is the path you are seeking. Maybe you are on the journey or you may be flipping leads. It doesn't matter. The process is starting with you in control.

ProActive Selling is all about this topic, and you may want to consider reading it if you are unaware of a good buy/sales process. These next steps should be an investigation method by both parties, not a "pitch and hope" like we see so often. Woof.

Next-Next Tool

The concept of being a step ahead is always a good one, and the next-next tool seems to cover it. Just don't think of your next step, think of your next-next step. Be it with your ATL buyer, your ATL, then BTL, then back to the ATL. Be it with your BTL the whole way. If you really buy into the buy/sales process, you should always be thinking next-next. Buyers want to be led.

Follow Up

It never ceases to amaze me how so many salespeople drop the ball on follow-up. The prospect says, "Call me in a month." Most salespeople forget to call in a month, and usually "Call me in a month" is an objection.

The follow-up is the best, lasting impression you can make to a call, showing that you are professional, value the prospect's time, and is a direct correlation to your company's products and services.

"Thank you for taking the time to discuss your challenges for the next year. As agreed, I'll follow up in a few weeks to chat about these issues again, and I'll give you a heads up so you can be ready. The next step is usually a fifteen to twenty minute discussion. Thanks again. Talk soon."

Professionalism usually wins.

OK, you are set. You are ready to tackle the world. You are prepared, you are ready, you have your sequences and templates. You are ready for the phone call, the emails, the objections. Practice the tools and, pretty soon, you'll be wondering why you avoided outbounding for so long.

PART 5

Sales Management: What You Have to Do

Coaching is the number one skill managers seem to lack confidence in, but is the number one skill that leads to salespeople becoming successful in their job.

—Skip Miller

Outbounding is not successful because salespeople are fearful, unorganized, and do not stick to a cadence. Period.

Another good reason outbounding is not as successful as it could be is because managers do not know how to manage, coach, and reward outbounding efforts. Period.

Outbounding is not the easiest thing for an SDR or a salesperson to do, so there needs to be sales management education, support, and guidance.

Typically, sales managers when they were salespeople were not that good at outbounding, so they have no successes to fall back on. Additionally, back when the sales managers were outbounding, a lot of the tools today were not available back in the good ol' day.

This is where management needs to be ProActive rather than reactive in helping the sales team obtain the goals needed to be successful. Focus on the things that cause results to happen, not just on the results. Here are some ideas.

CHAPTER 24

Develop the Process

Messages written at a third-grade reading level are 36 percent more likely to get a reply than those written at the college reading level.

A GOOD OUTBOUNDING process needs to be developed with the SDRs or the salespeople. An SDR/BDR process will be quite different than a salesperson's process, although the endgame, get a meeting and a next step, will be similar.

There are many different levels of outbounding.

- SDR Validate—SDR validates a lead and flips it over the fence to a salesperson.
- SDR Validate and Sell—The SDR can keep low-level leads and flip only the higher-revenue ones.
- SMB Outbounding—More transactional than most. Usually less than a one-day sales cycle.

- ▶ Commercial Outbounding—Typical outbounding motions to majority of prospects.
- ▶ Enterprise Outbounding—Usually more complex, higher revenue potential, and more touch points.
- ▶ Upsell Outbounding—Prospecting to current customers.

There are a host of derivatives for each one of these, but without a process, you end up managing chaos and are usually less effective than managers who have a process. The buy process needs to be looked at from the customer journey direction.

A PROSPECT'S BUYING PROCESS

Buyers buy in a process. We described this in *ProActive Selling*, and here is a recap. A buyer's process and a seller's process are similar; we just call them different names, since they are different processes. A buyer goes through:

- ▶ Initial Interest
- ▶ Education
- ▶ Validate
- ▶ Justify
- ▶ Decide

A seller goes through the same steps, but they call them different names.

- ▶ Initial Interest = Initiate
- ▶ Education = Discovery
- ▶ Validate = Proof of Concept

▶ Justify = Contracts/Purchasing
▶ Decide = Close

Staying with the buyer's terminology, the first step in that process happens when prospects have an *Initial Interest*. There has to be some beginning interest. People have an interest in a lot of things.

"I want to buy a new car."

"I want to buy a new TV."

"I need to buy a new software program for marketing."

Buyers have a lot of different interests. We all do. Interests are important. It's when prospects are motivated to do something about that interest that they start down a buying process. Being motivated moves a need from being static toward something they wish for or desire. It starts to come alive and have a life of its own. Motivation behind a need or desire is what causes *Initial Interest*.

Usually, this interest is because of a problem. An inbound lead, the customer usually has identified the problem. For an outbound lead, they may not have a problem right now, or do know they have a problem but one exists.

In any case, for a deal to go from Stage 0 to Stage 1, a problem usually has been identified. If the customer does not have a problem, you have no deal, period. It's that simple. If the prospect does not have a driving problem in the area you are discussing, there probably won't be any action (motivation) taken in the foreseeable future, since they have a host of other problems they are trying to solve.

If the prospects' interest level (problem) is high enough for them to continue their movement and to go to a next step, it's called *Education*.

Prospects, if they are motivated past the *Initial Interest* phase, will then want to educate themselves more on what they can do to

satisfy an initial need they have developed. Salespeople usuall
have this part down with feature/benefit- or feature/advantage
benefit-selling techniques. There are two education models tha
need to be addressed.

TWO EDUCATION PROPOSITIONS

There is the Technical Case/User Buyer Education. These are th
buyers who want to understand what you are selling, since the
are the ones who will be using it, praising it, complaining abou
it, and put in charge of making sure the company "gets its mon
worth" on this investment.

The Business Case/Fiscal Buyer Education is all about mone
Soft dollars, hard dollars, ROI. However the company is measu
ing success of the problem being solved (outcome) is what thes
buyers are interested in. Two different value propositions, an
you have to sell to both of these to be successful.

This is where the buyers take ownership of the solution offere
They need to *Validate* their education process. The best way
describe this is that there is a difference between a buyer who sa
"I get it," and when they say "I get it," and really mean it.

The first "I get it" is when the buyer fully understands you
product, its features, and its solution. They know what you a
offering, the features, and the benefits.

The second "I get it" is when the buyer starts thinking abo
how they are going to use it. How they are going to install it, sta
working with it, how life will be easier, they will be able to mal
more money, and so on. This is called *transfer of ownership*, or va
dation. Both buyers need to do this.

Once the buyer has completed the transfer of ownership,
unique thing happens. They start to think.

"Is this the right time to make a decision like this?"

"Have we looked at enough options?"

"Is this the right tool for us or should we look at a few more?"

Buyers, after completing a transfer of ownership and proceeding down the path to a decision, need to *Justify* their decision

Decide is the final buying step. If a prospect has gone through the buying cycle and are still motivated to reach this step, they will decide either yes or no. It is that simple. A buyer will say yes or no as a final step, then make the purchase (or not).

THE BUY/SELL PROCESS

Customers buy in a process. Understanding this process will help you manage backward into the process, will allow you to see clearly the direction your deals are going, and will enable you to hire the right people and create ProActive dashboards.

CHAPTER 25

Hiring Thoughts

Hiring the right team is the number one objective of great sales managers.

BEFORE YOU START looking at how to develop and implement a coaching process, you should look at your hiring process. Most companies hired salespeople over the past few years to follow up inbound leads. While still important, most companies are now looking at outbounding, and the skill sets for outbounding are very different that the ones for an inbound follow-up type of sales effort.

Develop a Profile of a Successful Performer so you can interview for what you need, not what you think you need. A Profile Sheet should be developed for each individual candidate. After the interview, grade the candidate on a scale of, check, check-plus, check-minus, or A-F.

You now will have a scorecard on the candidate and can evaluate on how they will perform against a success criteria, rather than what you think at the moment you need. Additionally, the candidate will know what is expected from them right up front.

You would be surprised on how many SDRs and salespeople get hired and after three months, what they thought the job was and what it has turned out to be is different. (Geez, I had no idea I was going to have to outbound so much. I just thought I was supposed to follow up on leads. At least that's what everyone told me.)

It doesn't take a lot of time to put one together, and the benefits are enormous. You will be able to:

▸ Put your thoughts down on paper
▸ Not focus on just one characteristic (Halo Effect)
▸ Not judge a candidate based personal appearances
▸ Not hire yourself (Cloning)
▸ Interview and hire based on objective metrics, not your gut
▸ Be consistent with each candidate
▸ Not just assume they can do it (Warm Body)
▸ Just hire someone who has done it before (Repeat Performer)

Profile Sheets are a must, and most managers who have hiring problems don't use them. Go figure.

Develop one that aligns to what you need, just don't copy this one. Change it up a bit every quarter. You need to have one, or you will be hiring subjectively and that's rarely a good answer.

Profile of A Successful Outbounding Sales/SDR

Job: Sr. SDR Sales Associate
Name:

Job Skills and Knowledge	Desirable Qualities
Wants to learn and grow	Persistent
Business acumen	Goal oriented
Selling to ATL and BTL	Empathy
Listening	Relationship builder
Objection handling	Time management
Communication skills	Following a predictable methodology

Five Characteristics Needed to be Successful
Naturally Curious
Self-Motivated
Organized
Quiet Confidence
Competitive

Background: Experience and Education	Will Enjoy Doing
Competitive background	Making customers money
Some sales experience	Doing what it takes
Success track record at anything	Really listening to customers
B experience	Doing the impossible
Multitask	
Sense of energy	

CHAPTER 26

Dashboards and Leading Indicators

If you can't measure it, why do it?

IN MY BOOK *ProActive Sales Management,* we cover two tools that can lead the manager into a process that is more proactive than reactive. It starts with knowing the formula:

R=F+C

Revenue, or Results, is a function of Frequencies and Competencies.

By just focusing on the results, you really are not in control of the things that cause the results to happen. The manager hopes that if they do a lot of stuff, the results will happen, which is like saying if the hamster runs faster in the cage, more results will happen, which is true, but there are limits to how much faster the hamster can go.

MEASURE LEADING INDICATORS— THE OUTBOUNDING MILLER 17

If you are familiar with *ProActive Sales Management*, you know about the Miller 17. If not, here is a quick overview of the Miller 17, which is a way to ProActively measure and coach behaviors. Following the R=F+C rule, here is an example of the Miller 17 for a normal sales team.

FIRST QUARTER REVIEWS–TEAM 1					
1–5 Scale (1 = Low - 5 = Excellent)					
	Bob	Mary	Jim	Debbie	Fred
PERFORMANCE	2.2	2.2	1.8	2.8	3.8
Sales Y-T-D	2	3	2	3	4
Sales Quarter Review	2	3	1	2	5
New Sales	3	2	1	5	4
Retention Sales	2	2	2	2	2
Margin Sales	2	1	3	2	4
SALES COMPETENCY	2.8	2.2	3.7	3.5	3.3
Sales Cycle Control	3	2	5	4	5
Presentation Skills	3	2	3	3	4
Sales Focus	3	3	3	3	3

FIRST QUARTER REVIEWS–TEAM 1 (continued)					
	Bob	Mary	Jim	Debbie	Fred
Product Knowledge	2	2	4	5	2
Efficient Resource Utilization	4	2	3	2	2
Customer Knowledge	2	2	4	4	4
FREQUENCY	4.0	3.0	3.3	3.5	3.2
Account Penetration	2	4	2	2	3
Territory Plan	4	4	3	4	2
Customer Support	3	3	2	3	3
Weekly Activity	5	5	3	2	2
Field Time Maximization	5	1	5	5	5
Calls Per Week	5	1	5	5	4

This grading scale shows "5" is way above expectations, 4—right on, 3—close, 2—we have to talk, 1—we really have to talk. Here is an example of the Miller 17 for an outbounding lead gen sales team.

SECOND QUARTER REVIEWS					
1–5 Scale (1 = Low – 5 = Excellent)					
PERFORMANCE	2.2	3.4	2.4	3.4	3.4
eads Generated	2	3	3	4	4
TL in Funnel	2	3	2	4	2
peline Activity	3	2	1	3	5
osell Activity	2	4	4	3	2

SECOND QUARTER REVIEWS (continued)					
Leads Converted to Prospects	2	5	2	3	4
SALES COMPETENCY	2.8	4.2	2.2	3.5	4.5
Sequence Standards	3	4	2	2	5
ATL/BTL Messaging	3	4	2	4	5
Changing Cadence Messages	3	5	2	2	4
Phone Outbound Skills	2	3	4	5	4
Persistence	2	5	2	3	4
Homework Skills	4	4	1	5	5
FREQUENCY	4.0	3.3	2.2	2.8	4.7
Using Homework	2	3	2	4	5
ATL Contacted	4	2	1	2	4
Pipeline Activity	3	3	4	3	4
Weekly Outbounding	5	4	2	3	5
Outbounding Time Management	5	4	2	2	5
Objection Handle	5	4	2	3	5

The Miller 17 is a report card working with the SDR and/or salespersons on measuring their plans and good intentions to outbound. If not graded, outbounding becomes a participation trophy sport, where no one wins or loses but gets points for just showing up . . . not a good idea.

The scale used here is the same 1 to 5 scale as the original Miller 17, but anything will do. The goal is to coach to Frequencies and Competencies, and the Results will be representative of that effort.

If you look at each rep, stay focused on the frequencies and competencies, you will be able to predict performance. This "report card" should be a coaching tool that the rep and the mangers work collaboratively on. Coaching to individual goals that align to company standards is what ProActive coaching is really about.

CT—THE CRITICAL THREE

Keeping salespeople and SDRs focused on weekly activity, and knowing the difference between important and urgent, is critical to their success, and the team's goals. The Critical Three is a weekly goal sheet to remind everyone of the difference between important and urgent.

Ask the salespeople and the SDRs to write down what is important for the month or quarter, and then weekly reports on progress. This is not a lot of time, and the results are stunning. What reps find out is how much time is spent on urgent stuff, and how little time is spent on what they know is important. Heck, everything is urgent, but moving the chains on the important stuff is what really makes a top performer.

• • •

What is the focus this week?

My Top Three

1. _____   Update_____
2. _____   Update_____
3. _____   Update_____

Team

Sales   Updates

1. _____   1. _____
2. _____   2. _____
3. _____   3. _____

Sales   Updates

1. _____   1. _____
2. _____   2. _____
3. _____   3. _____

Sales   Updates

1. _____   1. _____
2. _____   2. _____
3. _____   3. _____

Sales   Updates

1. _____   1. _____
2. _____   2. _____
3. _____   3. _____

The CT is a great coaching tool that keeps the sales team focused, without feeling they are being micromanaged.

CHAPTER 27

ProActive Numbers

ProActive wins games.
Reactive is looking at the game after it's over.

WHAT ARE THE key metrics to make sure the outbounding effort is going strong and the pipeline won't drop to zero? Here are the top five.

1. Time spent per day outbounding—at least sixty minutes to a maximum of four hours
2. Number of active cadences—depends on average sales price, but usually ten to thirty
3. Lead to prospect conversion rate (from Stage 0 to Stage 1, and Stage 1 to Stage 5)
4. Multicommunication mix (phone, social, email, and in-person outbounding)
5. ATL/BTL outbounding mix—a good 50/50 mix is hard but achievable

With these metrics, you can rule the world.

DASHBOARDS—QUANTITY AND QUALITY

ProActive Dashboards should track leading indicators, not just reactive ones like revenue. Dashboards should look at the activities that cause results to happen, and measure those. Basic metrics usually are:

- ▶ Open Rate percentage
- ▶ Click Through percentage
- ▶ Replied percentage
- ▶ Homework Call percentage
- ▶ LinkedIn Activity

Although most of these are looking backward, they still are important metrics to capture. Here are some examples.

Dashboard #1–Basic Numbers

Data From Jul. 1-Sept. 30	Total Calls	Call to Mtg Ratio	Meetings 2+ min.	Mtg to Demo Ratio	Demos	Demo to Sale Wins	Sales Won
Rep 1	2196	25.68%	564	8.51%	48	64.58%	31
Rep 2	1794	10.87%	195	11.28%	22	72.73%	16
Rep 3	1842	23.94%	441	4.31%	19	42.11%	8
Rep 4	1411	23.18%	327	10.09%	33	78.79%	26
Rep 5	2122	26.86%	570	2.98%	17	47.06%	8
Rep 6	1906	27.12%	517	6.77%	35	85.71%	30
Rep 7	1859	20.44%	380	7.63%	29	72.41%	21
Rep 8	1898	21.29%	404	6.93%	28	25.00%	7
Rep 9	2524	18.26%	461	7.16%	33	39.39%	13
Rep 10	1911	25.48%	487	7.80%	38	55.26%	21
Rep 11	1908	19.34%	369	10.30%	38	47.37%	18
Rep 12	1089	25.53%	278	11.15%	31	64.52%	20
Rep 13	1970	19.90%	392	9.69%	38	36.84%	14
Rep 14	2153	24.20%	521	11.32%	59	18.64%	11
Rep 15	2031	26.88%	546	2.56%	14	14.29%	2
Rep 16	2439	16.44%	401	8.73%	35	31.43%	11
	31053	22.07%	6853	7.54%	517	49.71%	257

Dashboard #2 – Basics

Here, the basics are covered, like opportunities created per month, how fast a lead was contacted, attempts made, and conversion rates.

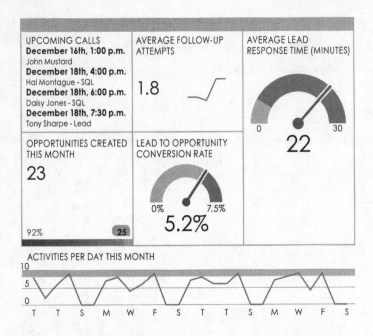

All good and basic stuff. Combine this with your Miller 17 and CT to have a forward and backward way of coaching your reps.

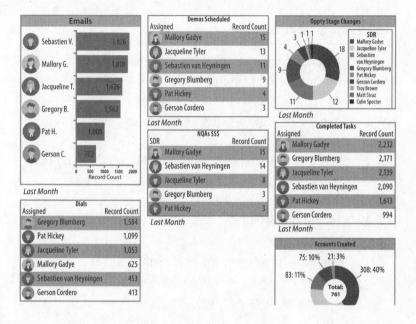

Other Coaching Ideas

1. Positive Actions—Measure the percentage or number of positive replies a rep receives, such as referrals, self-qualification, LinkedIn connects, or click-throughs.

2. Activity Outcomes—What are the outcomes of the actions required? Opportunities Created, Demos Scheduled, Connects Made, Meeting with AE, or actual Revenue Generated? Measure the Outcomes, not just the Activities.

3. Where to Improve—Remember, great coaches focus on positive actions, not just beat up salespeople because of failures.

Coach to the Process

Some random thoughts on coaching, since the topic of coaching could be a whole book in itself.

1. Effective Managers—They are consistent, they measure and coach to metrics.
2. Measure ProActively—How many ATL meetings, how many next steps, how many trumpets . . . whatever is needed at the time. See CT.
3. General rule—Outbound deals are usually bigger than inbound deals. Set the bar high.
4. What is the messaging you are leaving—Great managers coach their reps to develop great messages, not just give them a script.
5. Role Plays—Have the team create some role plays among themselves. Role play first calls, objections, and next step actions. Practice makes perfect.
6. Execution and being prepared are the organization skills that are needed the most, Salespeople are not born, and filling the funnel is the key, how to overcome the first objection, and be able to tell relational stories to the prospect to develop rapport.
7. Encourage the phone—I've seen way too many companies rely on emails and social only outbounding. Nothing beats using the phone.

CHAPTER 28

Putting It All Together for an Outbound Team

IF YOU ARE looking for a plan of action for an outbound SDR team environment, or even trying to get your AEs to start outbounding, here is a sample one for you to glance over. Again, it's one data point, but you may want to know what some best practices that are out there.

A plan should be defined as Inputs, Outputs, and Directive Coaching points. Those are some ProActive variable you can control and change based on the person you are coaching to.

• • •

INPUTS

A good way to start is to stack rank salespeople on inputs (calls, connects, emails, etc.) daily and/or weekly depending on the selling motion. This will make them compete with one another and help to diagnose their prospecting formula.

There is no universal formula. Some salespeople will gravitate to a more tailored approach through LinkedIn, and other reps will have a phone call–heavy approach. This could reflect the rep's strengths or it could be a by-product of factors out of their control like territory (geo, industry, etc.). The key is to provide them with visibility into the variables and then coach them around it.

You may want to incorporate input reports into SFDC dashboards so that you have a unified dashboard, but more granular input analytics are available in programs like Outreach or Sales Loft. That's where you can roll up the sleeves and get a better understanding of things like ideal call times, impact of subject lines on open rates, a/b testing emails, link downloads, and so on.

OUTPUTS

Generally speaking, solid outputs should be items like visibility into meetings that have been completed, meetings that are scheduled to go off in said pay period, and meetings that slipped (the scheduled date has passed and they are not marked as completed), and the like.

Regarding compensation, a simple two-component comp plan and have a 60/40 split between a higher-volume/lower-quality metric like meetings completed and a lower-volume/higher-quality metric like a specific opportunity stage. For the latter component, it is important to have visibility into not only the number of opportunities that have hit the stage that they get comped on, but also the number of opportunities that are queued up to potentially hit that.

COACHING

Most SDRs lack the business maturity to make sense out of dashboards to develop their own algebra equation. You may need to lead them to water in your one-on-ones and team meetings. Here's a three-step coaching process.

Step 1—Getting Them to Understand the Variables in the Formula

Hypothetical example:

Activity	Goal
Breakdown of where meetings come from	30% LinkedIn, 10% email, 60% call
# of calls/connect	10
# of connects/scheduled meeting	5
% of scheduled meetings that actually take place	75%
# of working days in the pay period	50
Meetings Target	30

Step 2—Getting Them to Understand Their Numbers

Numbers don't lie, and the best way to have salespeople accept their numbers is to develop a formula for each one. Here is an example formula for an SDR rep.

> Example: You need thirty meetings in the quarter–>You need to schedule forty (30/.75)–>You need two hundred connects in the quarter (40X5)–>You need to make two thousand calls in the quarter (200X10)–>You need to make thirty-three calls a day

Do the math, and the numbers fall out. There may be some slight variances, but at least you have a ProActive plan.

Step 3—Use a Comparative Lens

You want the salespeople to compare what they do with others so they can measure themselves. The need for team goals and averages is key from a coaching standpoint. Here is an example of how to coach using this lens with an SDR.

Comparative Coaching Example—John, it takes you ten calls to get a connect, but on average the rest of the team is getting a connect every seven calls (when are you calling, how often are you calling, etc.).

Coach—Explore differences and note outputs.

You are able to schedule a meeting on one out of every five connects, but the rest of the team is only able to schedule a meeting on one out of every eight connects.

Coach—Use questions.

▸ What are you saying on your talk track that is different than your peers that we can share?

PUTTING IT ALL TOGETHER . . . 303

▶ Who/ratio are you disqualifying?
▶ Are meetings being converting to qualified
   opportunities?
▶ Are you scheduling meetings with prospects where the
   SDR should be qualification harder?

Only 50 percent of the meetings that you schedule are taking place. The rest of the team is averaging a 75 percent conversion rate.

Coach—What can you be doing differently to improve your conversion rate? (modify calendar invite, improve qualification, call times, etc.)

You are clearly good at persuading someone to take a meeting. Even though you are consistently the lowest on the stack ranks for # of calls per day, you're still going to finish at the middle of the pack on meetings created.

Coach—What can you do so you are at the top of the stack ranks on calls this week? Do you think you'll have the most meetings created?

You make less calls than everyone, but 60 percent of your meetings are coming from LinkedIn and you are at the top of the pack for quota attainment.

Coach—Can you take point on sharing your LinkedIn best practices with the team? For you to learn and grow, it's important that you know how to use many communication devices, like the phone as well as social. What would happen if you paired up with (top caller) for a week to learn how they efficiently make dials?

CHAPTER 29

Summary

MANAGERS SHOULD USE the Miller 17, the CT, and Dashboards to measure the leading indicators as well as the trailing indicators for outbound activity and track velocity through their outbound funnel. R=F+C.

THE END

Managers, it's up to you. Great outbound sales teams can be tracked back to the managers. How well they hired, measure Pro-Actively, coach to outcomes and create a positive work environment. Rarely do salespeople want to outbound, but the best performers usually come from great teams, and that's a result of great mangers doing their job and setting standards.

Finally, a word about what employees want in their boss. Over the years, the data I see rarely changes. Employees want their boss to:

▶ Be Fair
▶ Listen and Communicate
▶ Be a Positive Influence

The only way I know how to do that is to be ProActive, manage to metrics, and reward when actions are met. You can do it. One step at a time.

Skip Miller
skip@m3learning.com
M3Learning.com

More tools can be found at: ProActiveOutbounding.com

INDEX

ABOUT THE AUTHOR

SKIP MILLER is Founder and President of **M3 Learning**, a Pro-Active Sales and Sales Management Training Company based in the heart of Silicon Valley. Skip has provided training to hundreds of companies in thirty-eight countries. He created M3 Learning to "make a salesperson better on each individual call." M3 Learning's signature selling methodology, ProActive Selling™, is unique in its high-definition focus on the *tactics of selling, creating value, and proactive sales cycle control.* His clients read like a Who's Who in technology. *Outbounding* is his seventh book.